HIP HOTELS
UK

HERBERT YPMA

HIP
HOTELS

UK

with 335 illustrations, 300 in colour

Thames & Hudson

contents

Tunel de la Tamise.

ILES SHETLAND

Echelles.

Tour de Londres au 16ᵉ Siècle.

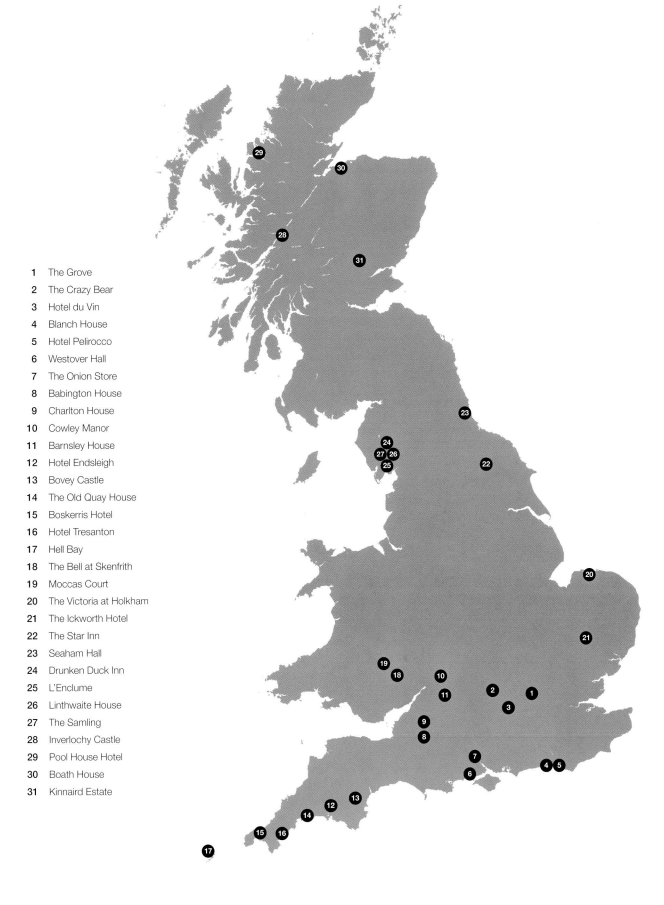

introduction

The enduring charm of the British countryside is what this book is all about. Not only is it beautiful and diverse, but it still supports a way of life that has not been modernized out of existence. It is still possible to find that little thatched-roof pub down a tiny lane nestled in a hidden valley. Or a completely deserted beach in Scotland, the likes of which puts most stretches of sand to shame. You can walk in the Highlands and not come across another person all day, and places like Dartmoor in Devon are so primordial that a time traveller from the 18th century wouldn't be able to tell the difference between then and now.

Tradition, natural beauty and a remarkably well-preserved way of life are the hallmarks of the British countryside; and yet, despite the impression that nothing has changed, country life in Great Britain is more modern, more up-to-date and more hip than any other countryside of any other country. And in true British style, this hipness is not always obvious.

The best two examples of thoroughly British tradition mixed with contemporary invention that are unique to Britain are the 'gastro pub' and the 'groovy grand' country house. It's a stroke of genius to take the very grand estates of British aristocracy and turn them into contemporary hedonistic retreats. Keep the signature Georgian architecture, sweeping lawns, classical gardens and bold vistas, and then add swimming pools, spas, bars and restaurants. It's all about the new luxury – space.

Equally brilliant but on a different scale are the gastro pubs: invariably tucked into picturesque locations, these are traditional inns where you can enjoy a pint of ale by an open fireplace, but when you take a seat in the dining room, the experience is fine dining of the white linen, bone china, silver cutlery variety, with a fusion menu to boot.

And round off the variety on offer in the British countryside, there are also the quirky places – strange little boltholes that celebrate their characteristic weirdness with style and panache.

oxfordshire and hertfordshire

At one time, Oxfordshire and Hertfordshire, together with Gloucestershire, Worcestershire, Shropshire, Cheshire, Northamptonshire, Leicestershire, Lincolnshire, Berkshire and Herefordshire, were all part of the middle kingdom of England called Mercia. The kingdom of Mercia began in AD 585. It was ruled by itinerant kings who moved continually from one royal district to another in order to live off their land as well as to demonstrate power and discourage uprisings. The local nobility were expected to feed and take care of these kings, which in itself was no mean feat.

One of the most well-known of these counties today is undoubtedly Oxfordshire, and in particular the University of Oxford. Teaching at Oxford first started late in the 12th century, and developed rapidly when King Henry II banned English students from attending the University of Paris. More recently, the University of Oxford has featured in just about every other film about something truly English, and yet despite all the obvious clichés, it manages to remain one of the best universities in the world, recently finishing third in a world-wide poll, just behind age-old rival, Cambridge, and Harvard in the US.

When thinking about Oxford, rolling green hills, villages with picturesque churches and brooks meandering along in the shade of weeping willows often come to mind. Summer skirts, bowler hats, cricket, Pimm's and willow hampers, idealizations all of them, yet to a degree they sum up the appeal of this part of old England. In fact, ensconced on a picnic bench in a stone-built, ivy-clad country pub, it's hard to imagine that the hubbub of one of Europe's largest cities is only an hour or so away.

Hertfordshire is even closer to London. Strange as it may seem, it is entirely possible to have lunch in the capital and within the hour be teeing off on a golf course with a world-class reputation – the city of London nowhere in sight. The counties flanking London have managed to avoid being wholly suburbanized. Of course there are pockets of suburban planning and building, but in between, the pristine charm of the English countryside is remarkably intact. Perhaps it's a reflection of how dear the countryside is to British sensibilities, but it is also a reflection of a nation where amongst land-owning families, primogeniture is the accepted hereditary practice, i.e. the eldest son gets the lot, and the endless subdivision of estates over several generations of inheritance is avoided.

the grove

For more than 200 years, the country estate of the Earl of Clarendon was a fixture on the social calendar of Great Britain. Prime ministers, royalty, actors, artists and London society all looked forward to much-coveted invitations to The Grove. Celebrated as one of the most prestigious houses of its day, and with the advantage of its close proximity to London, the hunting, shooting, fishing and tennis were as prized as the legendary largesse of Thomas Villiers – Earl of Jersey, British Ambassador to France, the first Earl of Clarendon and the proprietor of The Grove.

Two centuries later, surprisingly little has changed. The Grove is still one of the most popular weekend destinations for London society, and it has maintained its status as a venue for big society events, including the World Golf Championships in September 2006, which even if you're not a golfer is a big deal indeed. The attraction of The Grove today is very much the same as it was in the 1800s: the hospitality, its proximity to London and the fact that there is so much to do. With a world-class 18-hole golf course, a spa rated as one of the best in the UK, three swimming pools, tennis courts, mountain bike paths and extensive walking trails, there's not much that is not on offer at this estate.

But less than ten years ago it was a very different story. The last Earl of Clarendon had moved out in the 1920s, and The Grove had suffered the same depressingly familiar fate as many other hereditary piles in Britain. For a while it was a girls' school, and then a horticultural college and finally, in a 'how low can you go' scenario, it suffered the indignity of life as a training venue for – wait for it – British Rail. Apparently all of The Grove's boldly classical features, including enormous carved marble chimney pieces, intricate parquet floors and carved library niches were deemed impractical and of a distracting nature by British Rail, and as such they were plastered in. When the current proprietor found it in 1996, the interior of the house resembled a 1960s railway waiting-room (funny that). By this stage, the property had sunk into its last and final ignominy. It was a pig and chicken farm. Ten years later, the same pig farm is hosting the World Golf Championships. Looking at The Grove today, particularly considering it really is only forty minutes from the centre of London, it begs the question, why didn't anyone else think of this? With its 300 acres high on a hill in Hertfordshire, surrounded by mature trees, this is a 'proper' country estate.

Without shame, The Grove caters to the 'me' generation. It is hedonistic, from its rejuvenated Georgian roots to its new age spa juice bar. For culinary indulgence, there are three restaurants, not to mention the spa whose treatment menu is even more extensive than the restaurants'. But as much as it caters to the establishment's fondness for an indulgent lifestyle, it is certainly not establishment in its looks. The Grove is a new kind of grand: a groovy grand. From the outside it still looks like a traditional country house, but inside you will find no chintz, no plaid, no butler tables, no deep-buttoned leather anything, and definitely no paintings of cows or horses.

Instead, there is original art by Yves Klein, black chairs upholstered in lime-coloured cow hide and stainless steel four-poster beds crowned with feather plumes. And in this world of always having to plan ahead, with 227 guest suites, there's a fair chance that you will be able to get a room. But there are always those who pine for a world that's been left behind, and even these nostalgic types are catered for by The Grove. If you insist, you can travel to The Grove the old way; they will organize for you to arrive by river barge from central London via a series of canals that most of us didn't know still existed … just as long as you've got eight hours to spare.

address Chandlers Cross, Hertfordshire, WD3 4TG **email** info@thegrove.co.uk

telephone +44 (0)1923 807807 **fax** +44 (0)1923 294242

room rates from £280

the crazy bear

If you have a Drunken Duck (which we have, on page 206) then you have to have a Crazy Bear. And interestingly, the two properties have a lot in common besides their evocative names. They are both historic buildings that have developed rather organically from a traditional village pub to a gastro pub. These are places that have managed to retain the cosy ambience and approachable atmosphere of a 'public house' with the kind of food that one would normally find in a more formal traditional restaurant.

Tucked into a country lane – Bear Lane – in the tiny village of Stadhampton in the county of Oxfordshire, the 16th-century building was completely derelict when Jason Hunt found it in 1993. First job on the agenda in those days was to renovate the old inn. Downstairs, the old oak beams, fireplace and stone floors were rescued and restored, and upstairs, five bedrooms were converted into guest suites, but not in the style you might connect with a 16th-century stone building in Oxfordshire. Leaving convention behind and completely ignoring the predictable, the rooms feature zebra-pattern carpet, cobalt blue sinks and sculpted wrought-iron beds.

People, it seemed, were ready for something new, and the rooms were a big hit. They were followed by the creation of two restaurants, again with a fearless approach to their interiors. That's how The Crazy Bear ended up with a velvet-lined red-carpeted low-mirrored-ceiling den that must rate as the most avant-garde Thai restaurant in the British countryside.

Predictably, the decoration for The Crazy Bear's other restaurant designed in a more classic style is still equally unexpected; a shiny fire-engine-red room punctuated with brass studs like an old Chesterfield, sporting pink and red velvet chairs. Yet much as these spaces attract a lot of attention, it's the food that has made the pub's name. There's quite a culinary pedigree at what used to be known as The Bear and Ragged Staff. One of the partners, Nigel Sutcliffe, came to The Crazy Bear from the now famous Fat Duck in Bray, which as manager he was instrumental in getting off the ground (no pun intended).

Beyond the great food and the fearlessness of the design direction, the true signature of The Crazy Bear is its guiding philosophy. As Sutcliffe explains, 'we would rather talk about what we've just done than talk about what we're going to do'. That's what saw The Crazy Bear expand further in 2005, with the addition of five infinity suites.

Housed in yet another old building in what has now become The Crazy Bear complex, these are rooms that cater to people who are fond of the tactile. Rabbit-fur curtains, chocolate-brown mock crock leather floor edged in oak, mocha-brown glass mosaic-tiled bathrooms, crushed-velvet panelling, shiny deep-buttoned white satin padded ceilings and a gigantic bath set at the foot of the bed, disguised by a carved faux rococo Italian bed head.

Needless to say, these rooms have everything to do with the attitude of The Crazy Bear, and it's the Bear's attitude that makes it such a fun place to stay. In its commitment to organic growth, the latest addition is a fifty-acre farm next to the red London bus that functions as a reception. Yes, an old double-decker parked in a paddock is your first contact with the slightly mad pub. The new 'Bear Farm' also has a butcher, riding arena, stables and The Crazy Bear Farm Shop.

address Bear Lane, Stadhampton, OX44 7UR **email** enquiries@crazybear-oxford.co.uk

telephone +44 (0)1865 890714 **fax** +44 (0)1865 400481

room rates from £120

Fire exit ↑

hotel du vin

Even if you're not a 'rower', Henley hardly needs an introduction. Almost everyone has heard of the famous Henley Regatta – the annual boat race which has taken place between competitive yet amateur rowing teams since 1839. Yet despite the hype, Henley remains a charming unspoilt town on the river Thames in the rolling countryside of Oxfordshire. Each and every morning rowers bring their sculls, skiffs, sweeps and quads to the river's edge, and whether they row in rising mist on a summer's day or teeming rain in the winter, the atmosphere is one of a college town: quiet, refined, sophisticated but youthful. The fact that London is only an hour away makes it even more attractive.

Until recently, however, accommodation options in Henley were as traditional as the annual boat race. So the opening of Hotel Du Vin in Henley-on-Thames was exactly what the town needed; a relaxed quirky place to stay, with a true passion for food and wine. Following on from the tradition established by the previous six Hotel Du Vins of developing unique locations with style and flair, Henley-on-Thames's Hotel Du Vin was built into the premises of the old Brakspears Brewery on New Street – only fifty yards from the riverside moorings.

The result is a clever balance between the original features of the brewery and the requirements of a forty-three-room hotel. At first glance for instance, the red brick wall in the courtyard with its original Henley brewery signage looks entirely authentic. On closer inspection the windows are a recent addition, but the ones fashioned for this hotel are so appropriate to the building that they give the impression of being original. Inside it's the same story. The grand dame suite (all the rooms are named after wine labels and/or wineries) still has some of the brewery's machinery in its architecture – remnants of industry that function as sculpture of sorts. And the courtyard which once served as a loading bay for trucks is now a pleasant place for lunch or a drink on one of Britain's warm summer days.

From the beginning, with the first Hotel Du Vin in Winchester, a formula was established that is continued in each of the properties; an emphasis on the enjoyment of food and wine. Group founder Robin Hutson obviously learnt a lot about what's important to a memorable stay from his prior experience as manager of the Chewton Glen Hotel (voted 'The Best Hotel in the British Isles' by readers of *Condé Nast Traveller* magazine).

Being serious about wine, food and service is nothing new in the hotel trade, but the thing that makes this and every other Hotel Du Vin unique, is the way in which they manage to strike the right balance between being both elegant and laid-back. The brasserie that forms the nucleus of each hotel is completely devoid of the formality and pretension that can wreck a dinner. The food is good, the wine list is full of interesting choices without being in any way intimidating. Even if you know nothing about wine you can still enjoy the experience, and that's the well-orchestrated aim of the hotel. With a champagne bar and a brasserie that looks more French and more stylish than brasseries in Paris, it makes the choice of where to eat when you're a guest a no-brainer.

Strangely enough, even the French accent of the décor in the restaurant and bar is quite British. The English are the biggest foreign homeowners in France, and cross-channel tourist traffic is brisk. So all *ros bif* rivalry aside, it's really quite appropriate to Britain's newly emerging food culture to embody a bit of French flair and lifestyle.

And lifestyle is what the Hotel Du Vin is all about. All the rooms are equipped with flat-screen TVs and mini larders stocked with all sorts of goodies; the bathrooms are often as large as a standard hotel room, and the larger guest suites are packed with luxuries such as twin side-by-side bathtubs or a copper tub on a terrace overlooking the river – the kind of thing that would have seemed utterly outrageous in the UK just a decade ago.

Normally a hotel that is part of a chain would not necessarily fit into the HIP HOTELS quest for individuality, but in the case of the Hotel Du Vin in Henley-on-Thames, it really is different enough to be unique.

address   New Street, Henley-on-Thames, Oxon, RG9 2BP   **email**   info@henley.hotelduvin.com
telephone   +44 (0)1491 848400   **fax**   +44 (0)1491 848401
room rates   from £135

the south

The land that lies between London and the south coast of England is often referred to as 'The South', even though in truth, the counties of Kent, Sussex, Hampshire and Dorset have little in common other than sharing the coast of south-east England between East Anglia and Devon.

The modern counties of East and West Sussex are together almost the same in shape and boundaries as the ancient kingdom of Sussex. One of the Anglo-Saxon kingdoms in England, Sussex was a fiercely independent and powerful fiefdom that was almost continually at war with its Danish (Viking) neighbours to the north.

Sussex was, and is, blessed with rich farming land, but historically its greatest and most prominent assets were its vast forests. Even today, Sussex has the highest proportion of ancient woodlands in the country. In the late 1600s this forest of Andred, or *Andredswald* to call it by its original Anglo-Saxon name, exceeded 200,000 acres. It was a valuable source of timber, which fuelled the furnaces of the county's famous ironworks. Known as the furnace ponds, they survived as an industry until the 19th century.

It's not only the proud history of Sussex that has made it a magnet for people wanting to get out of London, but also the weather and the seaside.

Sussex has the highest annual temperatures in Great Britain, and the highest average days of sunshine. No wonder Brighton is billed as the Barcelona of Britain these days.

The appeal of Dorset falls into an entirely different category. Described as a stretch of Jurassic coast, Dorset's coastline was recently designated a world heritage site because of its geological land forms that include the splendid natural arch called Durdle Door. Many of the fossils found here, including fossilized Jurassic trees, document the entire Mesozoic era. Unlike the granite cliffs of Devon, the coast of Dorset is chalk and clay, which explains the extreme sculpting left by the sea and the formation of Poole, which claims to be the largest natural harbour in the world.

Again, it is neither Dorset's Jurassic heritage nor its coastline that has proved the main attraction. The primary appeal of Dorset, particularly for well-off Londoners, is that the county is not very populous and most of the land is still used for farming. That, teamed with some of the warmest summers and mildest winters in Great Britain, has made Dorset a big draw card for families who want their country retreat remote and unspoilt.

blanch house

Well-suited as Brighton is to the task, no one can rave forever. There was bound to be spin-off from its decade-long reputation as a party town, and those people who manage to wake up before sunset have long since realized what a nice place it is during the day, with its sea and its architecture and its laid-back attitude. Restaurants and bars have sprung up all over town, which now also cater to people who don't stay up all night. In short, raving is not the only scene in town, and Blanch House is three-dimensional proof of that.

Like Hotel Pelirocco, Blanch House can easily cater to the decadent and dirty lifestyle, but it also works for people whose idea of a great night out is cocktails and dinner, followed by more cocktails. For this you need a bar that does great cocktails and a restaurant that does great food, which is exactly what Blanch House provides. The bar – a long cosy space painted orange and crimson with long low benches and stylized Italian stools – is a serious cocktail bar. The barman is like a mad scientist, constantly experimenting with unusual combinations and trying them out on patrons. Then, when you're ready to get away from Doctor 'Martini' Frankenstein, you're led into the all-white dining room, sprinkled with works by local artists, for a sophisticated experience.

With dishes such as ravioli of butternut squash with oregano and blue cheese veloute by local chef Justin Anderson, it's the kind of food you would expect in London's trendier boroughs – which is what, in a sense, Brighton has become.

Blanch House is owned by Chris Edwardes and Amanda Blanch, a couple who have no doubt done their fair share of raving (and have the tattoos to prove it). To a degree they are representative of the new type of Brighton resident; street-smart, style-savvy and youthful in attitude. They are, in a word, hip, and their hotel is a direct reflection of themselves. It's also not their only venture in Brighton. Amanda Blanch has her own interior design business selling her distinct approach to interiors, and the couple have recently committed to transforming the Hanbury Ballroom in Kemptown, Brighton, into a private members club.

Food, drinks, interiors, nightlife: the one thing these diverse pursuits have in common is that they're all done with style. With rooms like The India Room dedicated to Rajasthan, the Art Deco-inspired Perrier Jouet room, and Galaxy Promises, the new top floor chocolate-brown suite – a James Bond-goes-clubbing kind of room – the delightfully decadent dimension of Brighton is still on show.

Other adult pleasures are now starting to sneak into the picture. With summers that last longer, and temperatures that require air-conditioning, Brighton beach is beginning to tempt bathers from June through to October. Sceptics might tell you that you still can't see the bottom, but the English Channel is definitely better suited to swimming than it once was in the past. Beaches, bars and restaurants all less than an hour from London – *ce n'est pas possible!* Who would have imagined, from the cold and grey pictures that typify old Britain, that Brighton would now be cultivating a distinctly Mediterranean lifestyle?

address 17 Atlingworth Street, Brighton, BN2 1PL   **email** info@blanchhouse.co.uk
telephone +44 (0)1273 603504   **fax** +44 (0)1273 689813
room rates from £100

hotel pelirocco

One four letter word has put Brighton back on the map and it starts with an 'R' not an 'F'. Throughout the 1700s and 1800s Brighton was one of the hot destinations for aristocratic London society. The esplanade was popular for parading on a sunny weekend, and the pier was one of the world's first amusement parks. The local architecture reflected the extent of the upmarket patronage. As Prince Regent George IV built his famous folly, the Brighton Pavilion, in high camp chinoiserie style, and just behind the beach, the waterfront is lined with row after row of immaculate Regency townhouses arranged in small squares not unlike their London counterparts.

There was also swimming, or more accurately, bathing to be done. This required the presence of a bathing cart, a wooden structure rather like a gypsy caravan that could roll right into the water so the bather would not be gazed upon as they submerged themselves in the sea. Then, as the motorcar revolutionized travel, Brighton began a long 20th-century down-cycle. It became semi-derelict and its only saving grace was that the rents were cheap.

In the late 1950s and early 1960s, drawn by the seashore, the close proximity to London and the low prices, Brighton became famous for its

mods and rockers, and for the clashes between the two. Then in the late 1970s and early 1980s it started to be discovered by creative types who couldn't afford to live in London. Performance artists, illustrators, out-of-work actors, sculptors and even famous DJs such as Fatboy Slim would make Brighton their home throughout the 1990s, planting the seeds of a revolution that was to catapult the sleepy seaside town back into the limelight: the rave revolution.

Brighton was perfect for getting on a train with your weekend rave kit in a bag, checking into a cheap hotel housed in the town's substantial collection of grand Regency townhouses, changing into glam gear and staying out at all-night raves pumped up by the power of various synthetic stimulants. Brighton became a nocturnal scene still best summed up by the words of Wilson Pickett: 'I'm a midnight mover – all night groover – I'm a midnight creeper – all day sleeper'. It was within this scene that Michael Robinson, a former DJ, and Jane Slater, a former PR girl, created Hotel Pelirocco. There is no beating about the bush with this hotel. It caters unashamedly to sex, drugs and rock and roll, albeit in an electronically-modified, 21st-century-rave format.

Even the bathrooms haven't escaped the cheeky sponsorship – this one is by Smint, the English mint with a funky image.

The Absolut Love room is sponsored by Absolut Vodka and if you look closely the chandelier is made up of tiny vodka bottles.

Each night, the bar is a scene in its own right. If you're a lazy raver, no need to leave the hotel.

...otel partly sponsored by different brands, ...nagery and presentation is often slick and ...rtaining. This is the cover of their menu.

The Dotty room by Yayoi Kusama rates as the most adventurous, and yet it has aged very well. It still looks fresh and fun.

A place like Hotel Pelirocco, with its crazy, irreverent mix of influences, would be incomplete without a nod to surrealism.

Situated in a townhouse in a Regency square on the seafront, in the centre of Brighton, the hotel is a handy staggering distance from the best clubs and bars, or you could stay in house at the hotel's Playstation bar, a hotspot in its own right.

Since opening almost a decade ago, the hotel has received only glowing reviews, even though its inspirations are hardly safe in decorative terms. It seems that people are harder to shock than anyone thought. Everybody has caught onto the idea that it's just fantasy. And, to paraphrase the Eagles, 'You can check out any time you like'.

Room themes range from the Pin Up Parlour dedicated to British blonde bombshell Diana Dors; Pussy, designed by Pussy Home Boutique; Modrophenia, an homage to mods; the Ocean Room created for couture clubbing couples and modelled on a VIP dressing room; and the Nookii Room which is based on the grown-up game for playful couples and features the trademark kinky bed, a strip show sign and lots of black satin. But the funkiest room, described as the ultimate dirty weekend suite, would probably have to be the latest edition to Hotel Pelirocco – the Durex Play Room. Dedicated to all things decadent and indulgent, it features an eight-foot round bed with a mirrored canopy, a separate living area, a giant plunge bath and of course, a pole dancing area. Painted hot-pink, it also has its own entrance (or maybe an escape) onto the street.

So there it is, an historic English seaside town transformed by one little four-letter word, and an adventurous hotel transformed by another.

---

address 10 Regency Square, Brighton, BN1 2FG **email** info@hotelpelirocco.co.uk

telephone +44 (0)1273 327055 **fax** +44 (0)1273 733845

room rates doubles from £95

westover hall

Westover Hall was once the beach house of the Siemens family – well known in Britain for their electrical appliances and fittings. But the only thing it has in common with most beach houses is that it is by the beach. The Siemens family was obviously not going to let some sand get in the way of living in grand style; so they ended up with a Tudor hall in the dunes.

Completed at the turn of the last century, the estate originally occupied five acres along the shores of the Solent, the name of the stretch of sea that divides the Isle of Wight from the mainland, and it was designed to be directly in line with the two outcrops of white limestone at the westernmost point of the Isle of Wight, famously known as 'the Needles'.

Of course in those days it was referred to as a 'marine residence' – possibly one of the finest of its kind built in England. Apart from its very carefully considered location, it was most remarkable for its total disregard for cost. Perhaps it wasn't the only marine residence with twelve bed and dressing rooms, three bathrooms (for the early 1900s that's a lot of bathrooms), a galleried hall, four reception rooms, a billiard room, a loggia and offices, but it was certainly the only one panelled in enough oak to build a fleet of ships.

The magnificent hall, a thirty-six by eighteen-foot space of great height is panelled like the finest Scottish castle, as is the vestibule, the library, the drawing room and the dining room. Throughout the ground level, most of the floor is also polished oak. From the custom-made brass hardware and extravagant use of oak panelling, to the highly decorative carved plaster ceilings and the leaded stained-glass windows, it is clear that this house was built with concern for quality, not cost, and estate agents handling the sale of this property in the early 1920s were keen to point this out. A hundred years later, the Siemens family's grand folly by the sea was still able to make a strong enough impression to convince the new proprietors to abandon their urban lives in London and move to the picturesque south coast full time in order to convert this marine mansion into a small but highly individual hotel.

Formerly a director at Storm model agency, Stewart Mechem was completely mesmerized by the potential of this stately beach house, and with his sister they set about its conversion. Because of the original family's largesse with space, the house proved particularly well-suited to conversion into a hotel, and as a result, hardly any changes have had to be made to the interior architecture.

Although the mansion no longer has the five acres of surrounding grassland, it still sits in the grassy dunes directly in front of the Solent. And the hotel is blessed with public spaces that overlook the dunes and the sea. There's the upstairs veranda, furnished in a casual rattan, and particularly popular as a retreat for afternoon tea, as well as the restaurant and bar (which doubles as a less formal space for lunch). The sea views are optimized by lots of glass. The Siemens family obviously considered the enjoyment of their view very carefully, and it's clear that the hotel benefits deeply from this. For people who prefer rolling waves and blue water to rolling green hills, Westover Hall is the perfect escape. Just like the Siemens family who were obviously sticklers for quality and attention to detail, the present proprietors are continuing the tradition and adding yet another layer of indulgence with a restaurant that has quickly earned a reputation as the best in the New Forest.

address Park Lane, Milford-on-Sea, Lymington, SO41 0PT **email** info@westoverhallhotel.com

telephone +44 (0)1590 643044 **fax** +44 (0)1590 644490

room rates from £200

the onion store

This surely must be one of the most eccentric hideaways in the whole of Great Britain. If you can find it that is.

Consisting of a collection of three former agricultural storage structures, namely a granary, an apple house and an onion store, the hotel is arranged along a tiny private gravel road on a farm deep in the heart of the Hampshire countryside. Even with detailed instructions, it's not easy to find, and that is part of the attraction. It's one of those places that fits perfectly into the notion of getting away from it all, and that is what has made it so popular. Each house can only accommodate one couple, so in terms of exclusivity you know you'll be sharing the entire property with a maximum of four other people. There is no restaurant, no bar, no lobby and no reception. Instead, there is the privacy of your own quaint little cottage and the luxury of no one knowing where you are or what you're doing.

There may be an absence of traditional hotel features, but that doesn't mean there's an absence of things to do. Top of the list (in terms of guests' favourites) is swimming in the heated indoor pool by candlelight. It's not what you would expect from a humble collection of utilitarian farm buildings, which makes it all the more fun.

The pool house, a kind of Bali-in-Britain greenhouse, with lots of plants, a glass roof and distinctly oriental furniture, is also where breakfast is served (again, for a maximum of six). In addition, one of the houses, the Apple Store, has its own Berber tent in its own tiny private garden, and at the other end there's a massive jacuzzi for two.

Without spelling it out, it's clear what kind of weekend The Onion Store is good for, but another part of the attraction is the proximity of nearby Romsey. One of England's best-preserved old market towns, Romsey is a pedestrian-only kind of town, with Elizabethan houses set on cobble-stone streets, plenty of charming old churches and the weeping willow-lined banks of the River Test. It's also packed with enough pubs and restaurants to provide plenty of choice in terms of places to eat and drink. The Onion Store will make some recommendations, but a lot of guests prefer to discover the area on their own.

And therein lies the magic of The Onion Store, it represents a new kind of escape – where the luxury is not a 'yes sir, no sir' style of pampering, but rather the notion of complete freedom and privacy. In short, there is no intrusion of any kind whatsoever.

The premise of The Onion Store is that as an adult you are perfectly capable of stepping into your car and finding a pub, and are equally capable of entertaining yourself in the absence of cable TV and in-room multimedia systems. The Onion Store is part of a growing global trend where in terms of getting away from it all, less is decidedly more. Left to your own devices, you might discover things to do that are normally superseded by virtual entertainment.

Staying here is a little bit like camping, but without the leaky tent or the mud, and of course it is still a hotel in the sense that there is someone to make your bed, clean your room and change your towels. The 'here I am, pamper me' hotel is still valid for a weekend escape, especially when you're not in the mood to make decisions. But getting back to basics can be fun, particularly when it's done in such an eccentric manner. And it has to be more effective than relationship counselling.

address Romsey, Hampshire, SO51 6DU

telephone +44 (0)1794 323227 **fax** +44 (0)1794 323227

room rates from £135 (2 night minimum)

somerset and the cotswolds

Somerset was famous the world over long before England emerged as a united nation. In Roman times, the town of Bath, known as *Aquae Sulis*, was one of the major religious curative centres of the empire. The city housed a vast bath complex constructed next to a massive temple dedicated to the goddess Minerva, to take advantage of the hot spring water that gushed out of the ground at a constant temperature of 46.5ºC (115.7ºF), as it continues to do today.

Rome was firmly in control of the agricultural and mining riches that Somerset had to offer, but had had to fight hard to get them, and it was a full-time task to stop the Iron Age tribes from taking back their lands. Eventually, the Romans needed both legions and funds to finance the fight for the beleaguered city of Rome itself, and thus they started to sell off imperial lands, thereby establishing a tradition of large land holding by rich gentry which remains in place to this day. Through wars and conquests over centuries, the names may have changed but the fact is that Somerset today remains a largely agricultural county. It is a place where the unspoilt beauty of the English countryside can be enjoyed in tandem with the convenience of nearby motorways.

The verdant countryside of the Cotswolds has a similar appeal. With their dark green rolling hills, densely wooded forest, idyllic little villages and beautiful estates built in locally quarried stone, the Cotswolds for many represent the arcadian ideal. Just as Provence has become the bucolic fantasy of people who dream of a house in France, the Cotswolds are the focus of many an alternative lifestyle plan. And like Somerset, the Cotswolds, despite being easily accessible via motorways, have largely resisted the flooding tide of modernization.

babington house

When Babington House opened in 1998 it was a complete revelation, or perhaps put more accurately, a revolution. Historic British country houses had been converted to hotels plenty of times before, but never like this. No one had ever taken a traditional Georgian estate with gardens and stable blocks, and turned it into a funky country hangout. Instead of chintz and antiques, Babington introduced cheeky modernity to the countryside, with design that doesn't take itself too seriously, but is still serious enough to be attractive.

But it wasn't just a simple case of changing the furniture or introducing new décor. The key invention of Babington House was lifestyle. Behind all the buzz and the hype created by its spectacular breaking of all the rules was the very simple and straightforward acknowledgment that country houses were out of step with contemporary life in general. Town and city dwellers were used to going to the gym, having breakfast late, eating what they felt like when they felt like, staying late to watch a movie and meeting for drinks in the bar. So why should they not be able to do the same in the country? It was the simplest question with a straightforward answer: why not indeed!

So in response, Babington opened with two restaurants, a wood-fired pizza oven, a gym, two pools and treatment rooms in the old cow shed (called Cowshed), family bungalows created especially for parents with children, and a bar that doesn't close until the last guest goes to bed. Traditionalists immediately dismissed it as inappropriate to the countryside, but in truth Babington House was being very traditional in the sense that the British have always escaped to the country for sport and recreation. And that is exactly what Babington is about.

Over the ensuing nine years, a lot has changed. What seemed like a radical step has now become almost the norm for country house conservation and revitalization, and in the process it has even picked up a nickname – groovy grand. But Babington House is still the first to lead the way, and it hasn't exactly been resting on its laurels. In addition to the fitness facilities, it also has a spa – housed in series of wooden cabanas which are spread out along the babbling brook marking the boundary of the property, and Cowshed has subsequently developed into a fully-fledged brand with a range of exclusive beauty products now increasingly available around the world.

Inside, a new cocktail bar has been introduced in what was once the library, and one of the restaurants, to cope with demand, has been extended onto the terrace enclosed in an orangerie that is open all year round, with views of the property's swan lake. Ilse Crawford, former editor of *Elle Decoration*, continues to upgrade many of the rooms in her signature eclectic style, not only keeping the whole experience fresh but also constantly improving the quality of lifestyle for members and guests. The signature power showers for instance – an enormous shower rose set into a corridor separated by a long wall from the rest of the bathroom, with very un-English water pressure – have been much copied. But no other hotel has yet been able to copy the comprehensiveness of Babington House's guest room facilities. This is still the only hotel in the British countryside where you could arrive without any personal effects (toothbrush, comb, hairbrush etc) without being inconvenienced. The attention to detail is second to none, and it extends to the electronic front too – each guest has a large flat-screen TV, a sound system (with thankfully no volume limit) and a cable TV service that offers something like 600 channels.

Babington House invented the notion of treating guests like adults, and it is are still a pioneer in this hospitality genre. The attitude is: so what if you're a TV addict or a late-night drinker. Babington simply provides a beautiful country venue for your own preferred brand of indulgence.

address Babington, Near Frome, Somerset, BA11 3RW **email** enquiries@babingtonhouse.co.uk
telephone +44 (0)1373 812266 **fax** +44 (0)1373 813866
room rates from £225

charlton house

The effortless casual style of Ireland in summer, the thrill of derelict architectural treasures, the bucolic lifestyle of the British countryside with its unchanged sports and traditions, the oriental fantasies so beloved of bohemian aristocrats: these are the themes that have provided Roger Saul with inspiration for the products in his Mulberry Home collection over many years. 'Irish Summer', 'Restoration', 'Pool Party', 'Country Life' and 'Bohemian Aristocrat' have informed the fabrics, furniture and accessories that make up Mulberry Home, and collectively, they form the decorative backbone of Charlton House. Mulberry is the quintessentially English fashion label founded by Roger Saul, which introduced a distinctly eclectic and slightly eccentric style via his series of boutiques. And with the exception perhaps of his own medieval home, Charlton House is the most perfect three-dimensional representation of the Mulberry style.

As much a bon vivant and bohemian connoisseur as designer, Saul's work has always been driven by his passions for historic architecture, for gardens, for the classic yachting scene and perhaps most of all, for exotic motorcars from the pre- and post-war years. These cars are the embodiment of the design optimism that inspired Art Deco in the 1920s and 1930s, and of the more scientific streamlining of post-World War II design. And he races them with all the passion of an early aviator. It's no coincidence that he identifies with his 'Bohemian Aristocrat' collection more than any other, because in a modern sense, that is exactly what he is. His is a style driven not by transient copycat ideas, but by passion and interest, the very elements that distinguish true aristocrats in the first place. As the legendary photographer David Bailey points out in his dedication to a book on Mulberry, 'Anyone can shop at Bond Street and copy something from a magazine, but very few people truly have their own style, and Roger Saul is one.' If the impression is that this story is more about Roger Saul the man than Charlton House the hotel, then that's exactly how it should be because the hotel is an extension of his own life and work.

Charlton House is a cosy jumble of massive Tudor carved four-poster oak beds, of rich velvets in oriental colours, of light breezy tea-washed chintzes in the style of Nancy Lancaster; of worn riding boots arranged by the fireplace, of blue and white porcelain and Georgian silver flatwear – all the beauty, tradition and quirkiness that the British countryside throws together with such conviction.

The last time I stayed at Charlton was in the late 1990s, and a lot has changed since then. A new wing houses a handful of new suites that are rather like having an entire stable house to yourself, indulging the guests with lots of space to go with the bohemian twist. Just as significantly, the hotel has added a wonderfully exotic spa named Monty's (after Saul's wife Monty), which could best be described as bohemian aristocrat on a health kick.

These days Saul is no longer part of Mulberry, having resigned as chairman in 2002, but the influence that inspired the label in the first place continues to play a role in the development of Charlton House. His latest passion, post-new hotel wing and post-new spa, is an organic farm called Sharpham Park, where venison sausages, pheasant burgers and spelt stoneground wholemeal flour and muesli are all part of a return to farm management on an organic level, and just as importantly, the results end up on the menu at Charlton House. Spelt in particular seems to be his focus, and don't feel bad if you don't know what it is, because the last time it was farmed in any significant quantity was about a thousand years ago.

address Shepton Mallet, Near Bath, Somerset, BA4 4PR **email** enquiry@charltonhouse.com
telephone +44 (0)1749 342008 **fax** +44 (0)1749 346362
room rates from £180

cowley manor

Deep in the heart of the Cotswolds, possibly one of the most English of all counties, lies a surprise. History and tradition are what you would expect to find as you wind your way along a classic, unspoilt narrow road through an agricultural landscape straight out of an arcadian scene from a Hardy novel. When the sign pops up pointing the way to the tiny village of Cowley, you might expect Cowley Manor to be one of those more English-than-English houses: a stately home with extensive gardens, estate cars, labradors, gun bags and an interior crammed with hunting scenes, padded wingchairs and deep-buttoned dark brown sofas.

The gate to the property doesn't give much away, with the exception of a neat cube of stone in one corner with the name Cowley Manor chiselled in a clean minimal contemporary typeface – a hint that this may well not be what you might expect. Arriving at the house, first impressions are of a well-preserved, very fine, very symmetrical stone pile in the very best Italianate tradition. A huge souvenir from someone's ancestor's Grand Tour perhaps. But then when you step inside, the classical picture deconstructs into a well-orchestrated case of bending all the rules.

Modern furniture upholstered in pink, lavender, yellow and khaki felt, funky lamps, contemporary sculpture and a purple billiard table in a deep-buttoned, brown leather room, with irregularly spaced turquoise buttons. Even the dining room, a grand ballroom-sized space panelled in exquisite wall-to-wall carved Louis XVI pearwood is furnished in lime green chairs with teardrop-shaped lanterns suspended from the twenty-foot high ceilings. Bathrooms feature immense showers tucked behind sheets of blue glass, and bedrooms are all white, with the odd accent wall of orange, pink or lavender.

It's as if the house – a Grade II listed villa built in 1855, which was once the home of Sir James Horlick, the malted-milk magnate – had fallen into the hands of a well-heeled aristocrat who spent his formative years in the heady atmosphere of Italy's forward-thinking design industry. Which, as it turns out, is not too far from the truth. Cowley Manor is the result of the passion of two young couples hell-bent on reinventing the classic English country manor. The story starts in London where Tim House and his wife Lucy were about to get involved in a hotel project with Mark Sainsbury, brother of Jessica, who with husband Peter Frankopan was also keen to set up a hotel.

That project, which resulted in The Zetter in London's Clerkenwell district, already had plenty of chiefs, and so Tim and Lucy shifted their ambition to areas closer to Oxford. When the Frankopans purchased Cowley Manor, which at the time was almost a ruin, they sought the help of Tim and Lucy, who came into the project as partners. Fired with the desire to create a new style of country retreat, they hired the up-and-coming architects De Matos Storey Ryan.

The results speak for themselves, but the process was greatly helped by the flexible approach of English Heritage. Bob Bewley, English Heritage regional director for the south-west, aimed for 'constructive conservation' in which a balance could be struck between maintaining the finest details of a historic building (and its gardens) and the merits of new architectural design and materials.

Elegant, simple and surprising are the words that pop up each time one wanders around the estate, admiring the result of a co-production between innovative architects, English Heritage and a quartet of visionary founders intent on confounding the usual country house expectations. Most impressive is that nothing seems an after-thought. They insisted for instance on a spa, and in doing so, created one of the best in England, even though its startling modernity is not readily visible, tucked as it is into the folds of the landscape adjacent to the old stable block.

With massive outdoor and indoor pools, you would imagine such a set-up would be hard to hide. Yet it's as subtle as the abstract chandelier in the entrance hall. The only criticism seems to be that Cowley Manor was designed so exclusively for city dwellers – yet ironically, in historical terms, that is the most traditional thing about the place.

---

address Cowley, Near Cheltenham, Gloucestershire, GL53 9NL **email** stay@cowleymanor.com

telephone +44 (0)1242 870900 **fax** +44 (0)1242 870901

room rates from £240

barnsley house

The appeal of Barnsley House is simple: great food, beautiful surroundings, exquisite garden. Let's start with the garden, which should surely feature on the agenda of every serious horticulture enthusiast. In 1952, David and Rosemary Verey inherited Barnsley House – a stone manor originally built in 1697 by Brereton Bouchier – from a family who had owned the village (of Barnsley) since medieval times. For the next five decades Rosemary Verey launched herself into a labour of love that eventually became celebrated as the exemplary way to tackle a small country garden. It was an unprecedented success for which Verey was awarded a Victorian Medal from the Royal Horticultural Society and an OBE from the Prince of Wales.

But more importantly, throughout the 1970s and 1980s, an entire new generation of gardeners looked to Barnsley House for a model of what can be achieved on a small scale. As Rosemary Verey readily admitted, she started out knowing very little about gardening and suggested quite convincingly that the only way to learn was to start planting. That, she said, was the only way you'll ever know the difference between *Buxus* and *Oxycoccus*, and the only way you'll ever be able to remember all those Latin names.

Eventually she became a gardening authority, author of countless books, a regular contributor to gardening columns for a myriad of magazines and newspapers and unofficial British ambassador of gardens to the United States, where the possibilities and potential of small plots were still in their infancy.

When Tim Haigh and Rupert Pendered bought the old village pub, a stone's throw from what had once been the village rectory, Rosemary Verey was still alive and her garden was being maintained by the gardener she had first employed years earlier. Sadly she passed away in 2001, and the Prince of Wales made a final poignant visit to her garden in 2001 after her funeral.

Tim and Rupert knew her family well and they discussed the possibility of turning the 17th-century house, with its medieval oak staircase, into a small hotel. Rosemary Verey's son had inherited the property, but could not envisage spending enough time to justify the expense of maintaining his mother's legacy. So in 2002 the house was sold to the proprietors of the village pub with covenants that the garden would not only be maintained to the standard that had made it so famous, but it would also be available for the public to visit, paying guests or not.

The arrangement has worked a dream. Richard Gatenby continues to work in the garden, maintaining a detailed diary as he does so, and the house is in better shape than it has been for decades, the result of a thorough renovation of the unseen boring bits (i.e. plumbing and electrics). Outside it is as it always has been: oak trees, sweeping chestnuts, limes and yew as planted by the resident rector in the 1850s, and the garden as started by Rosemary Verey in the 1950s. Inside it's a different story.

The new proprietors were on a mission to remove the chintz and all the other typical attributes that plague many English country house interiors. They kept the significant architectural bits like the 'grown oak' beams, the medieval staircase and the panelling in what is now the restaurant, and of course the stone fireplaces.

The rest was replaced with big floppy couches by Italian designer Antonio Citterio, and bath tubs designed by Philippe Starck. Walls are simply painted white. Very cleverly, in one swoop, the garden has become even more of a focal point of the house. The result is a hotel that combines the charm of a 17th-century stone house with the modernity and comfort of a loft and the luxury of a five-star hotel suite. Where else can you sit in matching bath tubs watching MTV on a flat-screen waterproof TV suspended between the two tubs, beside leaded glass windows that look out onto one of the most famous gardens in Britain?

Last but not least, the restaurant has made quite a reputation for itself, with a menu that focuses on fine ingredients and a delicate touch without being too grand … exactly, in fact, like the garden.

address Barnsley, Cirencester, GL7 5EE **email** info@barnsleyhouse.com
telephone +44 (0)1285 740000 **fax** +44 (0)1285 740925
room rates from £270

devon and cornwall

The Vikings and the Saxons conquered the east of England, but the west remained the land of the Cornish Celts. Even the Romans scarcely ventured past Exeter, the lack of safe ports and the wild moors of Dartmoor keeping them at bay. The Celts, who arrived in around 1000 BC, farmed the land and mined for tin, copper and iron, establishing a tradition that lasted well into the 1800s. A walk along the coastal paths or along the moors will even today bring you face to face with remnants of this British Bronze Age.

Only with the Norman conquest in 1066 were Devon and Cornwall for the first time fully integrated into England. Cornwall was given to the brother of William the Conqueror, and he built a dramatically sited castle in Launceston from which to rule the area.

But in the scheme of things, Devon and Cornwall never really featured very prominently in importance because the area was essentially considered to be poor and pestilent. Daniel Defoe, who published his accounts of a tour of Great Britain made between 1724 and 1727, described much of Devon as being wild, barren and poor. Tin-mining, however, remained an important source of income, until Great Britain's colonies provided opportunities for extracting ore more simply and on a far larger scale. Thus towards the tail end of Victorian times, the mining stopped, fishing declined, farming couldn't compete with the larger and better managed estates in the north, and the area went into a period of economic decline and neglect.

Ironically, it was exactly this isolation and hardship that helped to preserve the very things that now make the region so attractive. What both Devon and Cornwall have in abundance is unspoilt natural beauty, with splendid beaches and striking moors, salmon-filled rivers and a climate that is significantly sunnier and warmer than much of the rest of Britain. All the things that would have been razed by progress – the tiny villages, the old churches and cemeteries, the remnants of the Bronze Age and the open, unspoilt nature of the people – still survive. And now of course, they constitute the very reason that Devon and Cornwall have become exceedingly popular as an escape destination in Britain.

hotel endsleigh

In 1809 Georgiana Russell, Duchess of Bedford, set out to find a location for a rural retreat in Devon. This was to be a place where she could escape formality and live a simple life, as in the memories she had of childhood holidays in Scotland. Despite owning extensive estates in Cornwall and Devon, the Duke and Duchess did not have a house in the West Country and they decided it was time to build one.

She found what she was looking for in the Tamar Valley near Tavistock, a hidden piece of wonderful wilderness with steeply sloping wooded hills and a fast-flowing salmon river. It was here that she would be able to realize an outlet for her creative homemaking talents. She knew exactly what she wanted; a shooting and fishing lodge in the 'picturesque' style. Although often misinterpreted to mean merely pretty, the picturesque style was meant to evoke admiration. Endsleigh certainly did, and still does, that.

The architect Sir Jeffry Wyattville, one of the most successful and acclaimed designers of the day, managed to make a rather substantial house, complete with a separate wing for children, look like a gingerbread cottage in a forest. With oak tree trunks holding up the veranda and sheep knuckles embedded in the terrace floor to create

an outdoor stucco carpet, the design and decoration was pure fantasy. There was even an elevated children's pond, fed by water-spouting lions, to allow the Duchess to observe the children at play while she was in her study. The contrast between the rather wild, rugged setting and the delicate prettiness of the 'cottage orné' created perhaps the most charming example of the picturesque style in England.

Two hundred years later, it's remarkable how little has changed. The Tamar Valley is still hidden, undisturbed and wild, and virtually all of Georgiana's creative flourishes survive. Until recently, however, you would only have been able to enjoy the magic of this setting if you were a member of the Endsleigh Fishing Club. But even for a club endowed by the Duke of Bedford, the estate proved too demanding to maintain and fell into disrepair. From a distance, it was all still as conceived by Duchess Georgiana, Jeffry Wyattville, and the distinguished Humphry Repton, a student of Lancelot 'Capability' Brown and the most acclaimed landscape artist of his day – it remained a private Eden. But up close, the house was nowhere near as small as it appeared, and the interiors were suffering from a lack of care, attention and finance.

Enter Olga Polizzi, her husband William Shawcross and her daughter Alex. As Polizzi tells it, it was her husband who urged (insistently) for her to take it on – to save an extraordinary property from ruin, or worse, from falling into the wrong hands. With the hotel business in her blood (her father is Lord Charles Forte of the Forte Hotel Group, and her brother, Rocco Forte, is blazing a trail of his own with a string of luxury hotels) one would imagine another hotel would be the last thing she'd want to take on.

But she did, and her husband was absolutely right. She was the person for Endsleigh, and vice versa. The whole place was renovated; new plumbing, new wiring, new floors etc, and yet the impression is that with the exception of some new chairs and some modern art, nothing has changed.

It's a very clever smoke screen, because the reality is a starrily modern hotel offering every contemporary luxury that has still convincingly managed to disguise itself as an untouched historic property. Morph your favourite country pub, weekend fishing shack, cosy tea room and private hunting lodge into one, drop it into one of Devon's prettiest valleys, and there you have Hotel Endsleigh. Add the 'nothing is a problem' energy of Alex Polizzi and her informal attitude, and you have a powerfully seductive package. The restaurant is one of the best in Devon, the afternoon cream tea on the terrace or in the library is already a legend, and the guests themselves create an atmosphere thick with smug 'aren't we clever to have found this little piece of paradise' self-satisfaction.

address   Milton Abbot, Tavistock, PL19 0PQ   **email**   mail@hotelendsleigh.com

telephone   +44 (0)1822 870000   **fax**   +44 (0)1822 870578

room rates   from £200

bovey castle

Set in 368 square miles of Dartmoor National Park, Bovey Castle was built in 1906 for Viscount Hambledon, son of the founder of the WH Smith newsagent chain. With a father who made a fortune as a business baron, it's only appropriate that his private home – a beautifully situated estate – should be built in the baronial style.

On first appearances, Bovey Castle is the kind of ornamental stone pile usually found in Scotland. Although the galleried hall, acres of oak panelling and the exquisite vista of rolling hills is reminiscent of the Highlands, Bovey's strongest link to Scotland is via the ancient game of golf.

A golf course was built in 1926 at Bovey Castle as a sister course to those at Gleneagles and Turnberry. It was designed by J.F. Abercromby, the very architect who created the legendary courses in Scotland. The house and golf course represented the height of country luxury, but following the demise of Viscount Hambledon, Bovey Castle went into decline. For some decades it was a railway hotel owned by the Great Western Railway, and by the time Peter De Savary found it, the property had become a Le Meridian hotel, and in true soulless corporate fashion, most of the grand features had been boarded up or plastered over.

For De Savary, a veteran of challenges on such a scale, Bovey was a natural extension to his achievements at Skibo Castle in Scotland. An army of people went to work with a clear mission. This was to become the ultimate sporting estate in the UK. Anyone plucky enough to take on the challenge of the America's Cup as De Savary did in 1983, is obviously not short on confidence, and it is no doubt this total unshakable belief that saw the property completed ahead of schedule and on budget.

Purists might dismiss Bovey as not being a *real* castle because it was built as recently as 1906. But Parliament House in London is not that old, nor is it authentically gothic, but that doesn't stop it from being the most iconic and possibly the most photographed building in Britain. In any case, the point with Bovey Castle is not its history or the role it has played, or anything to do with its provenance. It is about being an extraordinarily comprehensive sporting estate, set in the grounds of one of the loveliest and most picturesque parts of Devon. The fact that it also happens to be blessed with a baronial (or neo-baronial) pile of ivy-covered granite designed in the style commensurate with the aesthetic expectations of a legendary 1920s golf course is a bonus.

Granted, the Art Deco-inspired interior mixed with Viscount Hambledon's baronial taste is a surprise, but an engaging surprise all the same. The 'Great Gatsby comes to England to play golf' look works very well, and it is totally in sync with a place that is destined to become one of England's top golf courses. But golf is only a fraction of what is on offer. With two all-weather tennis courts, a grass court, a trout lake, an equestrian centre, twenty-five miles of salmon fishing, an archery centre, a cricket pitch and practice nets, an indoor and outdoor swimming pool, saunas, steam rooms, a holistic spa, a crafts room, a clay pigeon shooting range and a falconry school, there is hardly a sport or activity that is not on offer at Bovey Castle. The emphasis is on experience, whether it's of something you know or something you might want to learn. In short, Bovey Castle is the Devon equivalent of a ski holiday, at least in the sense that you should sleep well at night due to severe exhaustion. For those who can still keep their eyes open at night, there's the oak room, the piano bar, the cigar cave and the palm court restaurant.

address   North Bovey, Dartmoor National Park, TQ13 8RE   **email**   enquiries@boveycastle.com

telephone   +44 (0)1647 445000   **fax**   +44 (0)1647 445020

room rates   from £295

the old quay house

It's pronounced 'Foye' but it's spelt Fowey. One of the oldest towns in Cornwall, the port of Fowey is famous for smugglers, pubs such as the King of Prussia and the trade in Cornish tin and fish and French salt and wine that has flourished here since the 15th century. What's more, the clay quarry just down the river was a source of fine white china clay much coveted by the likes of the Sèvres porcelain workshops set up by Louis XIV.

An indication of Fowey's historical status is that the largest ship in Henry IV's fleet was named the George of Fowey. With its snug harbour and old town chock-a-block with charmingly crooked, higgledy-piggledy buildings that lean every which way, some dating back to Elizabethan times, it's not surprising that the author Daphne du Maurier chose to settle here. Fowey has history and charm and character in spades, and despite the summer crowds it is still one of the most endearing seaside towns in England.

Bang on the water in the centre of town is The Old Quay House, built in 1889; a whitewashed piece of maritime history with its own dock and a terrace that once would have been the working place of the harbourmaster. More recently, it has been a hospital for down-and-out seamen. When Jane Carson and her husband found it, it was run down and in desperate need of a remake. The irony is, they weren't even looking for a hotel. They loved Cornwall, and were in search of a summer cottage. They were registered with an estate agent, and somehow by accident they ended up on the mailing list for commercial properties. So, back in London, instead of flipping through brochures and listings of houses, they ended up perusing commercial properties late at night in bed, and eventually 'maybe we could…' turned into 'why don't we…?' They sold up, moved to Fowey, and dived into turning the derelict boarding house into what is now one of the most stylish small hotels in town. Apart from its location, its trump card is the restaurant, arguably the best place to eat in Fowey. Style-wise, The Old Quay House is comfortably chic; a restrained but appropriately bright and simple approach that allows the view to remain the dominant feature.

In summer everybody stays on the terrace for as long as possible. It's a perfect spot for pre- and post-dinner drinks. Sticking directly into the town's bay, with a view of hundreds of sailboats bobbing on their moorings, this is the kind of place that makes you long to go to sea, but that makes most sailors want to drop anchor and come ashore.

SEAMENS

CHRISTIAN

FRIEND SOCIETY

HOME FOR AGED

&

PENSIONED SEAMEN

There's a healthy, sunburned, windswept, wholesome personality to Fowey, which you only find in towns popular with sailors. But you don't need a boat to be able to suck in the atmosphere; just a reservation at 'Q' Restaurant will do the trick. And considering the town's clamp-down on motorized traffic, a big advantage of staying at The Old Quay House is not having to schlep back up the town's steep hill to the municipal car park, hidden among the plane trees at the top. A short walk along the town's esplanade takes you to Readymoney Cove, a small and beautifully secluded beach which apart from being a perfect spot for a summer swim, looks out onto the ivy-covered remains of a medieval stone watchtower, a reminder of times when Fowey's status as one of the most important trading ports in Cornwall made it worthy of military protection.

address 28 Fore Street, Fowey, Cornwall, PL23 1AQ **email** info@theoldquayhouse.com

telephone +44 (0)1726 833302 **fax** +44 (0)1726 833668

room rates from £160

boskerris hotel

Perched high on a steeply descending hill, with the fine white sand of Carbis Bay beach only a short stroll away, Boskerris Hotel is a 1.5-acre property with a panoramic view of the whole of St Ives bay from St Ives harbour to Godrevy Lighthouse – the very lighthouse upon which Virginia Woolf based her famous novel, *To The Lighthouse*.

It's easy to sit on the broad terrace suspended above the kind of spectacular scenery that has made the west coast of Cornwall so famous, and be mesmerized by the beauty of it all. Boskerris Hotel and its setting remind me of Whale Beach, another steeply sloping stretch of beach an hour's drive north of Sydney. It too has great beaches, lots of families playing in the sand and some quite decent surf. Surf, surfers, turquoise blue waters, white-sand beaches and everyone within a four-square-mile radius dressed in board shorts and t-shirts: it's not your classic vision of the British coast.

Boskerris Hotel is a small fifteen-bedroom hotel that was the recent recipient of a complete makeover by Jonathan and Marianne Bassett, a young couple who wanted out of their London lifestyle. They found an alternative in the very place where one of them grew up.

This has been a hotel since the 1930s, but its state today bears little resemblance to the pokey, awkward guest house it once was. During the renovation, the number of guest rooms was reduced to make the hotel feel bigger and more comfortable, and to allow for the kind of bathrooms people now expect; i.e. with all the bells and whistles, and preferably by a famous designer.

There is an ethereal lightness to the Boskerris Hotel interior that works perfectly for a place with such a view. From the clean all-white dining room with its grey chinoiserie Chippendale chairs, to the slick bedrooms that would not look out of place in *Wallpaper** magazine, the Bassetts did a great job of matching the interior to the setting.

A twenty-minute walk from Boskerris is St Ives, one of the most vibrant and interesting towns in Cornwall. The artists of St Ives are well-known, and this old fishing port has become synonymous with the work and the careers of British Modernists such as Barbara Hepworth and Patrick Heron. But at one time or another, famous figures such as J.M.W. Turner, J.A.M. Whistler, Henry Moore and Virginia Woolf all lived in St Ives, drawn by the extraordinary clarity of the light and the rugged beauty of the cliffs, beaches and oceans.

From the terrace, Boskerris has an expansive view of St Ives, the surrounding local beaches and the Godrevy Lighthouse.

Gleaming damask silk, white linen, the odd bit of glass and lacquer: the bedroom décor is very much in the *Wallpaper** style

The all-white dining room, furnished in f Chippendale chinoiserie, serves a buffet lunch similar to that of Turkey and Gree

remove all trace of the depressingly
post-war hotel required much time,
money and effort.

Straightforward and unpretentious, Boskerris
has been a hotel in this idyllic location for ten
years, but only recently became so stylish.

The new owners are going to revamp the
ground floor, and in the meantime
have whitewashed it to get by.

With such a tradition, and the continuing presence of resident artists who come to the village for the same reasons as their famous predecessors, it's no wonder that the Tate operates an art gallery here. Known simply as Tate St Ives, this has been firmly recognized as the flagship of Cornish art since it opened in 1993. The gallery's block of modernity stands appropriately enough above the surfing beach of Porthmeor, and exhibits a collection representative of the modern St Ives school of painters such as Peter Lanyon and Sir Terry Frost.

The name St Ives derives from *St La* or *Hya*, the virgin Irish princess who according to legend is supposed to have floated on a leaf across the Irish Sea to these shores in the 5th century to convert the fishermen to Christianity. As a harbour, St Ives became important when Cornwall was exporting a lot of tin and copper. But my favourite story about its history dates from 1549, during the prayer book rebellion (a popular uprising against measures to replace liturgical prayer books in Latin with an English version) when the Provost Marshall came to St Ives to take the mayor Mr John Payne to lunch. Before lunch, he asked if the mayor could prepare the gallows and off they went for a meal at the Old Georgian Dragon. After lunch, the two men walked back to the village square, chatting gregariously all the way, and when they came to the square with the gallows that the Provost Marshall had requested, the mayor's guest insisted that the mayor mount the platform and slip a noose around his neck. He was duly hanged there and then for being a Catholic. It's the kind of cruel, gruesome story that can only seem palatable against the backdrop of Cornwall's blue waters and white sand; the kind of idyll that gives everything in life a more positive angle.

address Boskerris Road, Carbis Bay, St Ives, TR26 2NQ **email** reservations@boskerrishotel.co.uk

telephone +44 (0)1736 795295

room rates from £85

hotel tresanton

How times have changed. When Olga Polizzi first announced plans to convert the St Mawes yacht club into a small club-like hotel, the locals in St Mawes were not impressed. They didn't want a hotel, they didn't need one, especially not in cute little St Mawes, and all that noise and hubbub from city slickers was something they could do without. It was going to spoil their town.

Now almost eight years later, all the locals love the Tresanton. They frequent the restaurant so regularly it's difficult to get a table, and Olga is a hero to local homeowners because, thanks to her, property prices have tripled.

A lot of this inflation has to do with the recent emergence of Cornwall as a 'hot' holiday destination in England. Fowey, St Ives, Padstow, Falmouth and quite a few other coastal towns are experiencing a boom, but Hotel Tresanton has introduced something vital, namely the notion of style in a sustainable package. There is always a point in the popularity of a location where development becomes overdevelopment, and then the very things that made it so attractive – its unspoilt nature, empty beaches, quiet villages, beautiful views – disappear. That's the strength of Hotel Tresanton. It's exactly the right scale and attitude for a place like St Mawes, and because

the design is classic but contemporary, with a subtle marine twist, it's not likely to date any time soon. Thus, for people who are visiting for the first time, it's plenty new and fresh and modern, and for people for whom it has become a favourite, it stays the same. These are subtleties that point not just to Polizzi's experience as an hotelier, but to her experience in the hotel world at large. With a lifetime's exposure to the hotel business she has developed a keen instinct for the right hotel in the right place; and a particular sensitivity to things such as appropriateness, atmosphere, service and of course, the food.

Hotel Tresanton's restaurant started out, from the very beginning, with a reputation as one of the best places to eat in Cornwall. With time that reputation has grown. The Tresanton restaurant delivers the kind of quality you would not usually expect outside a big city, and that comes as a pleasant surprise for such a tiny place on the coast.

A house adjoining the hotel has been added to the complex and converted into three suites, one of which is perfectly laid out for a couple with a child: a parents' bedroom with a bay window and a view (of a bay no less), a corridor leading to a bathroom and a small study which could also be used as a kids' bedroom.

Light and breezy, furnished in neutral tones with a slight accent of lime yellow, they continue the tactile, clean-cut signature of Hotel Tresanton's guest rooms. But the biggest attraction remains the fact that Hotel Tresanton is bang in the middle of St Mawes. On a typical summer's day, children are digging for clams on the beach just below the restaurant's terrace, tiny sailboats are sprinting across the bay, while yet another handful of children might be found swimming towards the raft anchored off the beach. It's an idyllic picture and one that the Hotel Tresanton has been absorbed into as if it had always been a part of the scenery.

address   Lower Castle Road, St Mawes, Cornwall, TR2 5DR   **email**   info@tresanton.com
telephone   +44 (0)1326 270055   **fax**   +44 (0)1326 270053
room rates   from £230

the isles of scilly

They are often described as a cross between Cape Cod, Corfu and the Caribbean, and it's true: the water around the Isles of Scilly is as cold as Cape Cod and as blue as the sea in Corfu, and the beaches are as white as those of the Caribbean. Moreover, the air is free of pollution, the skies are a piercing blue, and the water is so clear that it is often difficult to tell how deep it is. And there's no trace of the milky blue-green that distinguishes most of Her Majesty's coastline as a result of rivers emptying into the sea.

Statistically speaking, this is the part of England that enjoys the mildest winter. In fact, it's often hard to believe you're still in Britain. But in centuries past, the beauty of these islands would have been in stark contrast to the hard life of the Scillonians. With little support from the mainland, the inhabitants scratched out a living farming, fishing and smuggling, and wherever possible, working as pilots to guide the big transatlantic clipper ships into nearby Penzance.

The fortunes of the islanders changed with the arrival of Augustus Smith, as chronicled in the story of Hell Bay (overleaf), and changed even further with the arrival of tourism. But one thing has not changed. Hell Bay, along with most of the west-facing coastline of the Isles of Scilly, is still among the most dangerous waters in the world. Although there are endless calamitous stories of ships in peril off the Isles of Scilly, one in particular is testament to the enduring notoriety of Hell Bay.

On 27 October 1929, an Italian ship became disoriented in the fog and ran aground on the deadly granite sentinels that surround the shore. The ship broke up and some of the crew drowned, but one lucky pantry boy was plucked from the foaming sea by Matt Lethbridge, a local who steered his gig – a large wooden boat rowed by six men – to rescue survivors. The Italian couldn't communicate with his saviour, but suffice to say he was thankful for his life. Local rescuers received medals of the highest distinction from Benito Mussolini himself.

Twenty-seven years later, history was to repeat itself in an eerily precise way. The ship's former pantry boy was now part of the crew on the ship SS Mando, which ran aground on the Isles of Scilly. Once again he found himself clinging to a piece of flotsam for dear life. And once again he was plucked from the icy waters by a Scillonian … Matt Lethbridge, the very same man who had rescued him from the sea over a quarter of a century earlier.

hell bay

While researching this book, two hotel names stood out as the most intriguing: The Drunken Duck and Hell Bay. Surely a place with such a name must, I imagined, be both dangerous and beautiful … and it is. The name is derived from the bay directly in front of the hotel, which is one of the most treacherous and infamous places for shipwrecks in the world.

Punctuated with a sentry of jagged peaks of granite poking through the wildly blue Atlantic surf, Hell Bay faces dead west and as such, is exposed to the full fury of the Atlantic Ocean. Countless clipper ships, steam ships, yachts and fishing crafts have foundered on these shores, generating enough hair-raising stories to fill an entire book.

Hell Bay certainly lives up to its name. In fact the island of Bryher has the distinction of having seen more shipwrecks than any other in the world. Dangerous yes, but it is also magnificent. It is difficult to imagine a more charismatic setting for a hotel, and it's hard to believe on a sunny summer's day with a Mediterranean sky and aquamarine water of the kind of colour you normally find in Santorini, that this is such a perilous place. But in nature, beauty and danger often go hand in hand (just look at a tiger).

Bryher is one of the smaller and least-populated of the Scilly Isles. There are no roads (unless you count the gravel path leading to the hotel), no cars or trucks (unless you include the hotel's Land Rover), and the total population of the island is around sixty. The island is wild, beautiful and untouched, and it still looks like what I imagine the rest of the world did a few thousand years ago.

There has only ever been one hotel on this island, and the present Hell Bay hotel is largely the creation of Robert Dorrien-Smith, a descendant of the man they used to refer to as the Emperor of the island. Since 1830 the neighbouring island of Tresco has been the private property of the heirs of Augustus Smith, a liberal-minded Freemason with a banking fortune, who was in search of a corner of England where he could implement his views on welfare and education. These were dangerous thoughts for a member of British aristocracy to have in the early 19th century, so Augustus Smith's move to the Isles of Scilly suited everyone. It was here that he built his family home in the style of a Scottish castle, using stone from his own local granite quarry, and then created one of the most exotic and famous botanical gardens in Britain.

Almost two hundred years later, a Smith (Robert Dorrien-Smith) still resides in a house called the Tresco Abbey, and Tresco the island remains the private property of the Smith family. The island of Bryher is just across the channel from Tresco, and at low tide it is sometimes possible to walk from one to the next. It's understandable that the family who have done such a stellar job developing their own island would be keen to do the same for their neighbour. The beauty of Hell Bay is that it remains rustic, wild and totally undeveloped, while at the same time offering splendid comfort and every conceivable luxury, including a heated pool, a spa, a sauna, a gym, a children's club house and very high quality cuisine. Guest rooms are spacious and the décor defers appropriately to the setting. The simple combination of wicker and blue and white creates a sort of basic beach shack chic.

But to a degree, it's almost irrelevant what the interiors are like, because on this island everyone is always outside. The collective land mass of St Mary's, Samson, Tresco, Bryher and St Agnes, is so small that the sky moves across at breakneck speed. It's British weather on turbo speed. Thus, unlike the mainland, even when it's cloudy it seldom lasts for more than a few hours, and the quota of sunshine is more Mykonos than the Midlands.

Best of all, and this is the quality that impresses most, is that with all confidence you can return to the island of Bryher some time in the future secure in the knowledge that it will not have changed. No one will have built a huge apartment block on the beach, nor will there be a casino or a nightclub, or an Irish pub. The local residents and the Dorrien-Smith family would just not allow it. Not many places on the planet can guarantee their own enduring charm.

address Bryher, Isles of Scilly **email** contactus@hellbay.co.uk

telephone +44 (0)1720 422947 **fax** +44 (0)1720 423004

room rates £260

south wales and herefordshire

A tiny county nestled against the border of south Wales, Herefordshire is not much different to look at from its neighbour. True, it's a bit flatter, but it has all the same charm and arcadian beauty of unspoilt valleys, rivers, forests and farms. In terms of its history, however, Herefordshire is vastly different from Wales.

When the Romans left Britain at the beginning of the 5th century AD, people had come to rely on them for order, structure and protection. Without the Roman armies, the people were left to fend for themselves against the fierce Picts and Scots from the north. Ironically, it was to the Anglo-Saxons from Denmark, northern Germany and Holland that the vulnerable Britons turned after the Emperor of Rome declined to send forces to Britain to help.

The Anglo-Saxon mercenaries who responded to King Vortigern's appeal noticed two things; the Britons were far from impressive warriors, and more importantly, their land was far more fertile than their own. Soon boatloads of Anglo-Saxons arrived, not to help the Britons, but to conquer them. The local population was driven to the border of Wales, which was inhabited by the Celts. Gradually, Britain was becoming English. Native Britons who resisted were killed or sold into slavery. Some escaped to Wales, Scotland or Cornwall.

When the Normans in turn seized their opportunity to invade in the 11th century, they brought with them an invention not seen before in England, namely the castle. Tiny Herefordshire became an important county because it represented the border between the conquered and the unconquered, the Anglo-Saxons and the Welsh. The Normans built castles as bases for raids into Wales, and established a castle-building tradition that was continued in subsequent centuries as Wales was gradually conquered over the next two hundred years.

Despite the best efforts of the Romans, the Anglo-Saxons and the Normans, the Welsh have managed to hang on to their Celtic culture. The Welsh language, recognized as one of the oldest in Europe, is still widely spoken in everyday life. Even the name Wales, from the Anglo-Saxon term waleas – which means foreigner – is testament that this land has always been different from the rest of England. With its mountains, castles and wetlands, its wealth of prehistoric remnants, and the stories of all its princely heroes who rose to claim the crown and give England its Tudor dynasty starting with Henry VII (Harri Tudur in Welsh), no wonder Wales has become the land of myth and music.

the bell at skenfrith

The Bell at Skenfrith is exactly how you would expect a cosy pub in Wales to be, including the name. Even though South Wales is really not that far from London, it gives the impression that it is much more remote. Part of this impression is created by the fact that all the signs are in Welsh as well as English the minute you cross the Severn Bridge. It may be part of the United Kingdom, but Wales even today works hard at keeping its own national identity, and people from England are sometimes viewed with the same mistrust as foreigners in rural France.

William and Janet Hutchings, the proprietors of The Bell, know this all too well. They may live and work in Wales, but they're originally from Somerset and Wiltshire, and they themselves can't explain exactly how they ended up in Wales. But the charm of The Bell and its fairytale location had a lot to do with it.

I had the dubious advantage of arriving at night – which from a navigational point of view meant I got lost three or four times before I finally stumbled across The Bell in the tiny village of Skenfrith (four houses and a church). The real plus of arriving at night, however, is that the next morning everything is new and different. And it was one of those perfect Indian summer mornings:

clear blue sky and a rising sun reflecting off heavy dew on the ground, with the pub standing completely by itself on a tree-lined riverbank, against a rolling backdrop of straw-coloured hills dotted with fat sheep.

The other poetic Welsh ingredient in The Bell's idyllic landscape is a castle – a wondrously foreboding ruin only two hundred yards from the pub. Started in 1160, Skenfrith Castle was completed in 1219 by Hubert de Burgh. But Henry III seized it in 1239 and passed it to his son who later became Edward I. Edward in turn granted it to his younger brother, Edmund Earl of Lancaster. Eventually it passed to John of Gaunt, whose son, Henry of Bolingbroke, deposed Richard II in 1399. He became Henry IV and the castle once again became a royal castle.

Three other castles are in walking distance of Skenfrith, namely White, Grosmont and Monmouth Castles. Henry V was born in Monmouth Castle, the same Henry who entered the history books with his spectacular battle against the French at Agincourt, immortalized by Shakespeare. The tourism committee of Monmouthshire County Council has produced a guide book called The Three Castles Walk in which it concurs that 'time seems to have stood still in Skenfrith'.

The village of Skenfrith was once known as Ynys Cynfraeth and was possibly named after a Welsh chieftain living there in the 6th century. With a history and setting like this, no wonder two English foreigners couldn't resist The Bell.

To their credit, the Hutchings didn't change much except the state of the place and the food. The old pub is now a luxuriously cosy inn, but more importantly, it has put itself on the map with its food. Janet Hutchings previously ran a catering business in London, and her culinary experience and passion are evident. She is not a chef, but it is clear that she has an almost instinctive feel for gastronomic quality.

Despite its remoteness The Bell has quickly built a reputation as one of the best places to eat in Wales, and as one of the top gastro pubs in the UK. But not too many pubs can offer an after-dinner 'constitutional' in a scenic ruin of a famous Welsh castle.

address   Skenfrith, Monmouthshire, NP7 8UH   **email**   enquiries@skenfrith.co.uk

telephone   +44 (0)1600 750235   **fax**   +44 (0)1600 750525

room rates   from £100

moccas court

Authentic is the first word that comes to mind. Tucked deep into the rolling countryside of Herefordshire, Moccas is an estate in the true tradition of a Jane Austen novel. Not just because the countryside is so English – even though ironically it's on the edge of south Wales – but because it's an estate that is still agricultural to its roots. Black-faced sheep still graze in the pasture separating the Norman church from the main house and much of the land is still leased to small farmers for crops. It is how it should be.

The first thing you see in the morning from your Georgian sash windows are the animals grazing beneath the massive oak, or the river Wye snaking through the property. These are arcadian scenes straight from the school of an 18th-century landscape painting, and to all intents and purposes one could still be in the 18th century because there is nothing at Moccas to suggest any different.

The view reveals no telegraph poles, no electricity cables, no motorways, no industrial parks and no high-rise buildings of any kind in the vicinity. It is the architectural equivalent of a micro-climate, a piece of unspoilt Britain which, as Country Life magazine will confirm with its ever ready statistics, accounts these days for less than one fifth of all British countryside.

Thankfully Moccas Court the house has the integrity to match its setting. Begun in 1775 by Sir George Amyand Bart, a wealthy banker who inherited Moccas through marriage to Catherine Cornewall, the sole heiress, Sir George went straight to the best to achieve a house suitable of his wealth and standing. Lancelot 'Capability' Brown drew up his garden and estate plans with assistance from Humphry Repton (two of the most legendary names in Georgian landscape architecture), and the famous offices of the brothers Adam were engaged for the architecture. Although the finished architecture is attributed to Anthony Keck, there's no mistaking the exuberant neo-classical signature of Robert Adam in the circular drawing room which today is used as a dining room, or in the magnificent oval cantilevered staircase of the salmon-pink hall illuminated by a spectacular domed ceiling of typical Adam-style decorative plaster.

Add in the nearby Moccas Deer Park, one of the three most important parklands in Britain, the sunken fern gardens traversed by a bridge leading to the original ice house, and the meandering Wye River which was once one of the best salmon rivers in England, and you have all the ingredients of a suitably grand country life.

An urn carved from pink marble
adorns the Robert Adam-designed
salmon-pink hall.

The true beauty of Moccas Court is its
authenticity. In every detail it is how you would
expect an English hereditary estate to be.

Through magnificent Georgian sash wind
guests wake up to a view of the grazing
on one side and the river on the oth

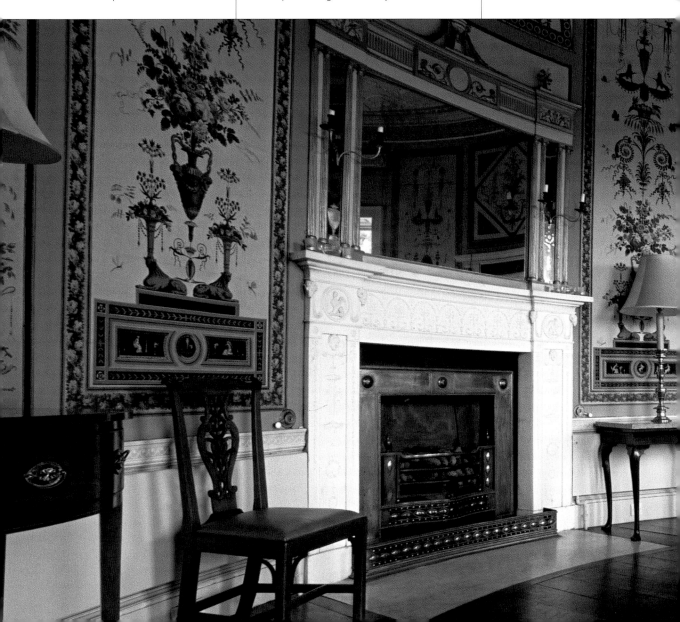

A decorative neo-classical detail from the Adam-designed round dining room.

Elegant but not grand, the guest rooms rely more on the architecture and the view to make an impression.

Baronet Velters Cornewall, the original proprietor of Moccas Court, hangs in the entrance hall in his finest brown velvet suit.

Predictably, as is so often the case with such properties, its fortune took a turn for the worse just after World War II, when the contents of the house were sold at auction (including 3,000 rare books from the library) and the house was let to a retired army colonel. Moccas was in a state of serious neglect when the father of the present owner, B. Chester-Master, took on the task of its restoration.

Interestingly, tragic as these dips in the life of historic estates can be, they nonetheless provide opportunity. Opportunity for the proprietors to reinvent themselves and for the traveller to experience something that was previously restricted to a small band of highly privileged aristocracy.

The true signature of Moccas as a hotel is the fact that it's not really a hotel at all. Not in the 'identical rooms along the corridor, cable TV and internet, and room service when you want it' style. Instead the things to do are no different than they were in Georgian times: a walk along the river, a visit to the Norman church, a picnic on the grounds, and at night cable TV is replaced by meeting for drinks with the owners in the library before sitting down to dinner in the seductive neo-classical surroundings of the round room. In a sense, Moccas has invented a new variant on country escapes, the pure historical estate experience. For the true fan of British country house history, it's an experience not to be missed.

address Moccas, Herefordshire, HR2 9LH **email** info@moccas-court.co.uk

telephone +44 (0)1981 500019

room rates from £140

east anglia

East Anglia is the bump of Britain; the large rounded piece that sticks out to the east. In fact its easterly position has shaped its history more than anything else. There is evidence here of human habitation dating back to 5000 BC (an abundance of found tools made out of flint attest to this), and of course the Romans had a presence, but the nature of Britain today as an Anglo-Saxon country has its origins in East Anglia's close proximity to Scandinavia and Germany, from where waves of Anglo-Saxon invaders arrived in the years after the Romans departed.

It also wasn't far for the Vikings to venture from Denmark, and they arrived in the 7th and 8th centuries in force. Wholly uninterested in the emergence of Christianity, they made a particular point of burning churches and destroying monasteries as they went about pillaging villages across East Anglia and the north of England. Eventually, however, the marauders became settlers, East Anglia quieted down and the proximity to other European nations such as Holland became an advantage, not a liability. Norfolk's extraordinary network of waterways, for instance, was perfectly suited for the corn trade that had been established with Holland.

The coast and harbour towns of Suffolk were equally busy. But it was inland that the value of this area made its mark. Once the vast oak forests were systematically cleared the land proved to be fertile, and being relatively flat, it was well suited to agricultural development.

In Norfolk for instance, the original Viscount Coke, the one who built the magnificent classic Palladian pile called Holkham Hall, was one of the first big land owners (43,000 acres) to introduce modern farming methods.

At one time, Norfolk and Suffolk were among the most densely inhabited areas of England, but as society shifted further west, and more specifically, west of London, East Anglia's population went into decline. Which is exactly why it is seeing such a resurgence today. The gently rolling hills of Suffolk, with its gingerbread Elizabethan cobblestone towns, and the vast beaches, extraordinary coastline and sweeping dunes of Norfolk have made these two counties two of the best kept secrets of the east of England. A lot of people still think of the area only in terms of its flatness, which suits the people who have discovered its unspoilt charms very well indeed.

the victoria at holkham

Since its reopening in 2001, following a lightning six-month renovation – or more accurately transformation – The Victoria at Holkham has created quite a buzz. According to the press, it is England's answer to the Hamptons, which is pretty accurate given the youngish laid-back city crowd that have made the north coast of Norfolk hip.

But the Hamptons are overcrowded and expensive; East Hampton is full of ridiculously expensive Swiss watch shops, and what used to be farmland is now crowded with overblown mansions, squeezed onto plots that were once potato farms. Then there are the traffic jams, a regular occurrence particularly on the weekend. In these respects, the north Norfolk coast has nothing in common with the Hamptons. And you certainly won't find a place like The Victoria anywhere on Long Island.

So what exactly is the buzz about? First and foremost it would have to be the location. Situated at the top of an oak-lined lane leading directly to the beach, the Victoria is a stone's throw from one of the most amazing stretches of beach in the United Kingdom; a massive expanse of dunes with grass-edged sandflats and adjoining pine forests, the kind you would more expect to find on Cape Cod. The fact that horses are allowed on parts of the beach is another plus, and the beach is so vast (seven miles long and in parts over half a mile wide) that even on the busiest days you still have the impression of having it all to yourself. Imagine that in the Hamptons on a busy July weekend.

Then there's the pub itself. When the lease came up for renewal on what was by then a slightly down-at-heel corner pub, Viscount Coke, heir to the vast 25,000-acre Holkham estate, recognized as one of the best-managed agricultural properties in the country, decided that he and his wife Polly could do a better job. Sidestepping the usual sprinkling of second-rate antiques and lots of busy chintz that constitute the interior design of most country house hotels, they redid the whole place with container-loads of stuff from Rajasthan. Village daybeds have become informal couches, colonial four-posters can be found in the bedrooms, old trunks serve as storage or a place to sit and ancestral portraits hang on emerald-coloured walls. The result is exotic and eccentric, and yet perfectly appropriate to the Victorian era of the building, paying homage to Queen Victoria's reign at a time when there was great fascination for exotic pieces from far-flung corners of the Empire.

Laid-back is how the Cokes wanted the place to be, and in this they succeeded, especially in terms of the restaurant and bar. As a result, at lunch and dinner the atmosphere is decidedly un-British – in fact it is quite Italian, with lots of families, lots of food and lots of noise.

Indian furniture, rich colour, Italian ambience alla famiglia; this mixture of unexpected styles and surprising influences is oddly consistent with the history of this family. Thomas Coke, the first Earl of Leicester who built Holkham Hall – billed as the most classically correct Palladian house in the country – wanted a showcase for his paintings, sculptures and drawings following the completion of the Hall in 1764.

This was the first time an aristocrat of grand standing had made such a gesture, an extraordinary act of openness almost two hundred years ahead of the trend. This openness and interaction have continued as a family trademark through the generations, and radiate from The Victoria today. The pub is a thoroughly unstuffy place where the welcome is neither disingenuous nor overly inflated. Balance is something the family is good at, and balance is the key to The Victoria's attraction. It is not too formal, not too casual, the food is great but not tortured in the way many restaurants in desperation for a Michelin star are prone to be, and the rooms are funky and fun without being silly.

address Park Road, Holkham, Norfolk, NR23 1RG **email** victoria@holkham.co.uk

telephone +44 (0)1328 711008 **fax** +44 (0)1328 711009

room rates from £100

the ickworth hotel

'A stupendous monument of folly' is how Lady Elizabeth Hervey, wife of Frederick Hervey, Earl of Bristol and Bishop of Derry, described her husband's plans for a new house on the Ickworth Estate in Suffolk in the early 1800s.

By any measure it was an ambitious undertaking, a 104-foot-high classical rotunda flanked on either side by a curved gallery the length of a football field, leading to two symmetrical wings, east and west, each the size of an entire palace. Building a property of such palatial proportions would be enough to test anyone, but to do it all by correspondence from Italy was the type of wonderful madness for which the Herveys of Ickworth have been famous for more than three hundred years.

It's true that the Bishop, who spent most of his time travelling rather than tending his flock in Ireland, initiated the monument that the Hervey family are identified with. But other Herveys before and after also contributed to the reputation – or some say the curse of – the Herveys. There was Lord Hervey of Ickworth, second Earl of Bristol, who was so effeminate and promiscuous, and of such ambiguous sexuality, as to inspire Voltaire's immortal line: 'When God created the human race, he made men, women, and Herveys'.

Any family that can illicit an aphorism from a figure as legendary as Voltaire is obviously newsworthy, and so the Herveys have remained ever since. The library, the dining room and the rotunda are hung with painted portraits of ancestors, each with a wicked story to tell. There was Augustus John Hervey, the third Earl of Bristol, the son of the subject of Voltaire's quote, who distinguished himself with a career in the Royal Navy, and had a reputation for womanizing on a scale to outdo Casanova.

In more recent times, there was Victor Jermyn, the sixth Marquess of Bristol, Earl of Leicester, and proprietor of Ickworth Estate, who turned to burglary to supplement the family's fortune. Unfortunately for Victor he was caught stealing jewels in Mayfair and sent to jail. Emerging from his infamy as a born-again aristocrat, he thereafter immersed himself in the company of monarchs and royalists loyal to crowns that no longer existed.

By far the quietest of all the Herveys was John Augustus, son of the Bishop and the fifth Marquess of Bristol, who completed the folly begun by his father, and managed to move his brood in and turn the monument (which the Bishop only intended as a container for his art collection) into a family home.

Sadly, the Hervey/Ickworth story ends with the seventh Marquess of Bristol, who squandered the family fortune on heroin and sold the remaining hold on Ickworth – a ninety-nine year lease renewable in perpetuity – to the National Trust, before dying of a drug overdose. Apparently Frederick, the current Marquess of Bristol (son of Victor Jermyn), is none too happy that he has no house to go with the title. But for fans of stylish weekend breaks, the downfall of the Herveys was a stroke of good luck. The magnificent 1,800-acre estate in the heart of Suffolk is now for paying guests instead of royal acquaintances.

But not all of Ickworth is a hotel, only the east wing, which was the family's residential quarters. The rest of the house (the curved galleries, the rotunda and the west wing) is operated by the National Trust, creating one of the most unusual hybrids I have encountered: namely a hotel that is also attached to, and part of, a museum.

Beyond the impressive grandeur of Ickworth's imposing land and architecture, the hotel is modern and relaxed. It may be grand, but it is definitely not formal. The bar is open twenty-four hours a day, there is an orangerie for breakfast, a brasserie-style restaurant for lunch and informal dining, and a trendier one for dressing up at night. The style is 1960s rococo: an eclectic mix of colour with the odd antique housed in a Georgian architectural envelope.

There are no room numbers. Instead all the rooms have been named after characters in the Hervey world, and as we have seen, the Hervey family was certainly not short of protagonists. With an indoor pool, riding stables, a garage full of mountain bikes, a football field, and an entire walled garden filled with toys just for the kids, Ickworth has no shortage of things to do.

The family may have been mad, but no one could ever accuse them of having no style.

address   Horringer, Bury St Edmunds, Suffolk, IP29 5QE   **email**   info@ickworthhotel.co.uk
telephone   +44 (0)1284 735350   **fax**   +44 (0)1284 736300
room rates   from £185

yorkshire, northumberland and county durham

The history of Yorkshire and neighbouring Northumberland and County Durham are inextricably linked to that of the City of York, which has been the commercial, financial and political capital of the north of England since Roman times.

With their knack for choosing splendidly well-suited sites for their cities, the Romans began their campaigns of conquest in the north here, building a fortified city that could permanently house an army of 6,000 legionaries, as well as room for commerce and industry within the walls of its protected fifty-acre compound. Ships could sail to York via the Humber Estuary, and then onto the tidal River Ouse, making it an important and thriving hub of trade. With olive oil, wine, red Samian pottery from Gaul, tableware from Germany and grain and horses for the army, it was not unusual to find merchants from as far away as Sardinia in this sophisticated stretch of Yorkshire. So important was *Eboracum,* as it was known then, that the Roman Emperor Septimius Severus settled here in AD 208. Constantine the Great, the first Christian Emperor and the one who declared religious toleration throughout the empire, was in

York when his father passed away and his troops proclaimed him successor to the imperial title.

Four and a half centuries after the Romans abandoned Britain, Yorkshire came under the rule of the Vikings. The Great Heathen Army, under Ivar the Boneless, landed in East Anglia and pushed northwards, defeating the king of Northumbria at the Battle of York in 866. The Vikings renamed the city *Jorvik*, and their fiefdom was, for a time, three times the size of Yorkshire.

Under the rule of the Vikings, the wealth of the surrounding countryside was truly exploited. The forests of Yorkshire and Northumberland provided plentiful timber; iron ore and copper were mined for the metal-working industry; and the fat of the land – sheep, cows and goats – made Jorvik an exporter of substance, establishing trading links with the Mediterranean, the Middle East and other parts of Great Britain. Even after the last Viking king, Erik Bloodaxe, was killed and York was absorbed into the rest of England, Danish customs and law-making remained in place. Rich, powerful and independent: these have long been the hallmarks of this picturesque northerly part of Great Britain, and they remain so today.

the star inn

Tucked into the prettiest part of Yorkshire on the edge of the North Yorkshire moors, not far from Castle Howard (possibly the most charismatic of all English country estates), is The Star Inn: a 14th-century thatched inn that continues to uphold a 600-year tradition of authentic rural hospitality.

The building is the type American magazines inevitably wax lyrical about. It is what they would describe as a fine and typical example of a cruck-framed long house with low beams, candlelit nooks, padded pews and big open fires. Originally these long houses featured a byre (a cowshed) at one end – now The Star Inn's dining room – and a dairy at the other – now the pub's front bar – with a fireplace in the middle.

Situated in the tiny village of Harome just outside historic Helmsley, the original name of the pub was The Board Inn. Despite its remote location this rustic thatched public house (the name changed to The Star in 1890) has enjoyed quite a reputation. It won the Egon Ronay Pub of the Year award in the early 1970s under different landlords. But The Star Inn has really lived up to its name in the past decade, ever since Andrew and Jacquie Pern took over as proprietors. The catalyst for their stellar success was the cooking of Andrew Pern. In this he juggles the traditions of his northern roots with English classics prepared in a manner that has much in common with legendary French chefs such as Marc Veyrat of the Haute Savoie and Michel Bras of the Auvergne, who both created an international sensation by focusing on recipes and ingredients true to their unique locales.

Since the beginning, Andrew Pern's combination of 'poet' and 'peasant' in one menu has attracted the kind of accolades and trophies that most chi-chi restaurants of big cities can only dream about. *Departures* magazine described his cuisine as 'stylish English cooking that balances grand flavours with surprising delicacy'. The Star Inn was voted Gastro Pub of the Year in 2006 by Egon Ronay, and not surprisingly it was awarded a Michelin star in 2001.

With The Star Inn set on a parallel path to its counterparts in France, the desire for a hotel started to take shape. Most of the famous three-star establishments in France have their own hotels – Troisgros, Michel Bras, Michel Guérard, Alain Ducasse and Marc Veyrat. There's a good reason for this: after enjoying a magnificent meal and superb wines most people would really rather not climb back behind the wheel of a car.

Thus in 2002 the Perns were delighted to be able to acquire a handful of traditional farm buildings across the street to create a lodge to complement the pub. With eight spacious guest rooms, a splendidly rustic round dining room and a double-height lounge, the lodge continues The Star Inn's strategy of combining tradition with invention. Style-wise, the hotel is impossible to pigeonhole: the Cross House Lodge is a thoroughly original mix of rustic ingredients such as old beams, open fires and hunting trophies with contemporary flourishes like hand-wrought staircases and bathrooms constructed in heavily textured reclaimed timber. The result is North Yorkshire rural with an edge.

To round off the experience, the Perns also added a store called The Star Inn Corner Shop which they describe as a 'north country deli', packed full of local produce and an abundance of home-made delicacies. Recently a third cottage was introduced to the complex which adds another three suites to the accommodation potential at the inn.

All in all, it's hard to imagine a more attractive alternative to drinking and driving. You might even walk away with their recipe for Baked Ginger Parkin with rhubarb ripple ice cream and hot spiced treacle. In fact it's on page fifteen of their brochure…. Now that's a *liberté* even the French would be hard pushed to match.

address Harome, Near Helmsley, North Yorkshire, YO62 5JE **email** starinn@btopenworld.com
telephone +44 (0)1439 770397 **fax** +44 (0)1439 771833
room rates from £140

seaham hall

Almost every morning at around 8:45 am it's the same story. A noisy gaggle of enthusiastically excited ladies and the odd guy start to arrive at the reception of the Serenity Spa. At 9:00 am the doors open and the crowds shift into the Ozone restaurant for a herbal tea or freshly squeezed juice before the treatments commence. It reminded me of school or university, with the kind of energetic chit chat that precedes the start of lectures. Except in this case it's not pursuit of knowledge that people are interested in; instead it's out-and-out hedonism. A whole day of being pampered, massaged and manicured, along with a break for lunch. I've seldom seen a spa with such buzz, but then I've seldom seen a spa of this scale in Britain. Set in its own modern, vaguely Asian-style building, the place is as extensive as the treatments and therapies on offer.

Seaham Hall is not just a hotel with a spa, it's a spa with a hotel. Voted best UK spa by the *Guardian*, best UK retreat by *Condé Nast Traveller* Reader Awards, and the world's best spa for style by the *Sunday Times Travel* magazine, it's not surprising that people travel from all over the UK to visit the Serenity Spa at Seaham Hall. It may not be terribly practical for Londoners, but the facilities are an incentive and it does have a helipad.

The key phrase at the spa is 'day ritual'. This is not a clinic where you arrive for a treatment and a cup of ginseng tea and then go – the whole day is an experience: from lunch in the orientalesque Ozone restaurant, overlooking the hotel gardens, to a pause in the Zen room, intended for no other purpose than the tranquil contemplation of your treatment and for the clever introduction of other treatments on offer via a mini sampling such as the mini manicure and the mini pedicure.

The only question is how did a place like Seaham Hall, with a spa where the fitness centre alone is of a higher calibre and standard than any to be found in Greater London, come to be on a quiet and remote stretch of the County Durham and Northumberland coast? The answer is all to do with Tom's plane. Tom Maxfield, the proprietor of Seaham Hall (as well as The Samling), made his fortune in computer software, and apart from indulging in his pleasure of investing in highly individual hotels, he is also a keen amateur pilot. And it was while flying along the north coast of England from his own nearby estate that he first noticed the rather forlorn but nonetheless impressive proportions of a property that once must have been a rather grand estate.

Pale, refined, minimal: the Ozone restaurant
is a suitably appropriate blank page
– to highlight the food.

Inside the spa, the circular, Asian-inspired
restaurant is the hub of a day
at the Serenity Spa.

The Serenity Spa, an extraordinary fre
standing modern complex, is consiste
voted one of the best spas in the U

...architecture is Georgian, but the guest ...ooms are refreshingly contemporary and free from clutter.

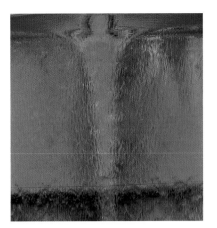

The hotel entrance is distinguished by a whirlpool in a massive glass tank – a funky take on a traditional fountain.

Situated in a remodelled historic Georgian family estate, Seaham Hall combines 18th-century grandeur with contemporary design.

Seaham Hall was the house of Sir Ralph and Judith Milbanke, the parents of Annabella Milbanke, wife of Lord Byron. As with almost every other grand family estate in 20th-century Britain, the property became unsustainable and was eventually used as a sanatorium. By this time the gardens hardly existed, and the once rather splendidly proportioned Georgian stone building had been modernized and renovated so often it was hard to find any original bits worth saving.

Undeterred, Tom Maxfield and his wife Jocelyn, who is responsible for the interior design, focused on the strengths of this unusual property. One, it was located directly adjacent to a ruggedly attractive portion of the north English coast; two, it was somewhere quiet and remote enough to be almost devoid of traffic; three, you could see the stars at night; and four, it was conveniently located if you happened to live in York, Leeds, Newcastle or Manchester.

Because there was not much left to save, and as a contemporary approach seemed more in line with the plans for the adjoining spa, the design direction of Seaham is one of rich modernity: clean lines and pared-down geometric shapes, executed in richly textured fabrics and warm bold colours. The resulting statement suggests a difference, without sacrificing the warmth and cosiness that can make a bar and salon inviting and attractive.

Great care and consideration was also given to the fact that, particularly in this part of England, the weather is not always conducive to strolling around the grounds. Thus an elaborate subterranean curved tunnel with a floating deck hovering above a pebble-lined internal river leads to the spa, with a magnificent bronze elephant trumpeting your arrival. This, in a nutshell, is not just any spa. And that might well be the defining statement of Seaham Hall.

---

address Lord Byron's Walk, Seaham, County Durham, SR7 7AG   **email** reservations@seaham-hall.com

telephone +44 (0)191 5161400   **fax** +44 (0)191 5161413

room rates from £225

the lake district

It was one of those summers that occasionally hit the British Isles. Countryside that's normally many different tones of emerald green had been fried to the colour of straw and was more consistent with the landscape of Tuscany than that of England. There were water restrictions in place everywhere and the famous British lawns were left to turn to hay. It was all decidedly un-British – until we arrived in the Lake District.

It was raining when we arrived, when we left, and most of the time in between. And everybody, particularly the Brits, was loving it. Surely this was what England was supposed to look like in the summer? Impossibly lush and green, with an ever-changing sky, the odd glimpse of sun and lots of cosy pubs nestled into the folds of the countryside. And then of course there are the lakes; elegant, finger-shaped slivers that anchor the valleys of the stone mountains in a series of magnificent reflections. Add to that the old wooden steamships that still ply the waters and a handful of picturesque yachts, and you start to understand the attraction of the Lake District.

But even its abundant charms didn't quite explain the thousands, literally thousands, of Japanese tourists. Why specifically the Lake District? The answer was provided by a local who explained that when the Japanese learn English at school, they start with Beatrix Potter, whose books are all set in and around Lake Windermere. Peter Rabbit, Flopsy, Mopsy, Cotton Tail, Hunka Munka, Tom Thumb, Mrs Tiggywinkle – the hedgehog dressed as a washerwoman – and of course, grumpy old Mr McGregor, all hail from these parts. And in the land of the rising sun, a pilgrimage to their home remains a powerfully enduring nostalgic fantasy. As a result, particularly in summer, the roads around the lakes are clogged with traffic. But it has not been spoilt. There are no shopping malls or amusement parks, and the furthest the locals seem to have gone to cash in on the area's publicity is to tart up the odd pub. Head down any hedge-lined lane and you won't bump into a soul, even though it's hard not to remark how it reminds you of the adventures of Peter Rabbit.

drunken duck inn

You have to love a place called the Drunken Duck Inn. It looks exactly as you would expect – cosy, approachable, cute as a button, with a dark, welcoming bar and a rustic white dining room. It's the kind of pub you dream about finding; the old local on the corner that hasn't been spoilt yet. But this old local has a view that you won't find in many corners of the globe. Situated adjacent to Hawkshead, this pub is on the top of a peak that folds down into a successive series of green valleys, with the rocky peaks of the Lake District mountains in the background. Toss in a few healthy brown cows and lots of sheep, and you start to get the picture.

But the cleverest thing about the Drunken Duck is that it still looks and feels like a country pub, and from first impressions you would never guess that it's one of the most celebrated restaurants in the north of England, nor that it has its own brewery, which is selling its own ale all over the Lake District and beyond, and least of all that it's a hotel with seventeen softly sophisticated rooms that are attractive enough to be almost always booked out in advance.

Neither would you guess that there's a tarn – a spring-fed mountain pool – in the garden, and an even larger one just a short walk away.

Nor would you know that all of the pub's water, including that for its own brewery, comes from its own source.

There are a lot of facets to the Drunken Duck Inn, all of which help to amplify the experience, and all of it came about the old fashioned way, i.e. slowly. Thirty years ago Stephanie Barton came up to the Lake District for a holiday job and stayed for the next thirty years. Marriage and children made her rethink her approach to her local: two decades ago, the only food served was chicken and chips in a basket. But then the advent of more approachable, affordable venues in London and other English cities inspired her to reinvent the Drunken Duck Inn as a gastro pub.

The same story goes for the brewing; starting literally with bits of old brewing equipment they bought and put together, Stephanie and her husband now sell a couple of hundred barrels a week to other pubs around the British Isles. Despite all the developments, however, the appeal of the Drunken Duck Inn remains the ambience, style and attitude of the idyllic little English pub. And the story behind the name of this pub is told on a board kept in the front bar: one day, a barrel of beer broke its hoops and the ducks drank the contents which spilled out into the yard.

When the old lady who owned the pub came onto the street, she was struck by a sight she had never seen before: a whole bunch of ducks flat on their backs in the middle of the road. Convinced they were dead, the old lady quickly set about plucking the ducks ready to roast. Only then did the ducks wake up with no feathers and in a hurry to fly away. As the story goes, she felt so guilty for scaring these poor birds that she spent the winter knitting them all little jumpers, and named the pub in their honour. Which only leaves the question, do ducks get hangovers?

address   Barngates, Ambleside, LA22 0NG   **email**   info@drunkenduckinn.co.uk

telephone   +44 (0)1539 436347   **fax**   +44 (0)1539 436781

room rates   from £110

l'enclume

L'Enclume is situated in the tiny picturesque village of Cartmel, a place known for its beautiful stone priory, its sticky toffee, and for Simon Rogan's Michelin-starred restaurant.

Although it is in the Lake District, it is nowhere near the lakes. That, depending on your own preference, can be a big asset. It means you are far enough from the crowds to be able to enjoy the charm of a classic village in Cumbria, but also that the coast is almost as convenient in distance as Lake Windermere (twenty minutes either way). In any case, given Rogan's fast-ascending reputation in the British world of fine cuisine it is safe to assume most visitors make the journey for the food.

Cooking in a style restaurant critics call 'ultra-modern continental', Rogan draws from his ten years experience of working with Marco Pierre White, John Burton Race, Keith Floyd and Jean-Christophe Novelli, to turn out inventive dishes such as flaky crab and caramelized calamari (try saying that quickly), pavé of Angus beef with a parsnip and star anise purée and a coulis of apple, and desserts such as a coconut soufflé with mango chutney ice cream. In fact the inventiveness of the kitchen is so acclaimed that most guests opt for the tasting menu even though there is an à la carte. It's not gastro-science like The Fat Duck, but it is very creative nonetheless.

At first everyone in the eye-gougingly competitive world of haute cuisine was surprised that Rogan would choose a site so far north. But if France is anything to go by, all the most acclaimed three-star restaurants are also the most remote. People, it is clear, are prepared to travel for a culinary experience. And perhaps the travel even enhances the enjoyment because any voyage, no matter how short, tends to heighten the senses and expectations.

If it was a pub, L'Enclume would be considered the latest contender in the growing British phenomenon of gastro pubs, but in fact it used to be the village smithy. *Enclume* means anvil in French, and the anvil still sits in a niche in the wall of the restaurant. The old oak beams have been cleaned up, the walls have been white-washed, and the rustic irregularity of this old workshop lends a lot of charm to the restaurant. As a plus, a small river runs through the property (a blacksmith always needed to be near water), and in summer it is possible to dine next to this babbling brook and gaze upon Cartmel's much-admired stone abbey, which is just on the other side of the water.

L'Enclume is really a restaurant with some guest rooms rather than a hotel with a restaurant. In the firm tradition of some of France's greatest chefs (Michel Troisgros, Michel Bras, Alain Ducasse and Mark Veyrat) the idea is to provide rooms for guests who are too blissfully satiated to contemplate driving a car after a pleasurable palate experience.

With L'Enclume's taste and texture menu comprising up to twenty dishes, and easily qualifying as an all-night affair, it's not hard to understand why the creation of guest rooms was a logical and much-needed step. The rooms are divided between two houses that flank the former 800-year-old blacksmith workshop, and there's also another house in the village that can sleep eight. As can be expected from such a small individual place, each room is different, ranging from the butter yellow Print Room to the Garden Room that opens straight onto the river. L'Enclume has without doubt introduced the tiny Cumbrian town of Cartmel to people who had certainly never heard of it, very much in the tradition that has seen Padstow in Cornwall being called Rick Steinville. Remarkably, only five per cent of L'Enclume's business is local, and the rest is drawn from other parts of England and beyond. No wonder the adjacent farm field had to be hurriedly made into an impromptu helipad.

I'm not sure whether being in 'the sticky toffee pudding capital of the universe' (the *Guardian*'s epithet for Cartmel, not mine) is good for a restaurant such as L'Enclume, but I am sure that most people making the pilgrimage haven't given it a moment's thought. Besides … you can buy a Cartmel pud at Fortnum & Mason.

address Cavendish Street, Cartmel, Near Grange and Sands, LA11 6PZ **email** info@lenclume.co.uk

telephone +44 (0)15395 36362

room rates from £89

linthwaite house

If I was asked which hotel has the best view in the Lake District, it would be a toss up between The Samling and Linthwaite House. Both have spectacular vistas of Lake Windermere, and both are perched high on the hill to provide a panorama of Britain's largest lake with the moor-like mountains of Cumbria as a dramatic backdrop. Both hotels were designed to maximize their view, The Samling a century earlier than Linthwaite House. But ultimately I think Linthwaite House has the edge because at this former Edwardian villa, with its distinctive black beams on a white exterior, you have the impression that the view is entirely yours.

The hotel's fourteen acres of woodland and rolling hills are so successfully hidden in the landscape that there is no trace of the multitude of tourists that crowd the Lake District. No traf.ic noise, no sign of the tour buses, no hint of the hustle and bustle that goes on at the lake's edge. Supremely tranquil, beautifully tucked away, Linthwaite House is a magic spot that conveniently has a hotel on the premises so that you don't have to leave the enchanting view.

Luckily, the hotel is perfectly in step with the view. Not in the sense that it is spectacular, but in the sense that it is equally snug and enveloping.

Cosy without being stuffy, luxurious but not pretentious, Linthwaite House is unexpectedly casual and remarkably comfortable. As a guest you feel that you're staying in someone's house and that the owner of the house is a genuinely happy host. Which when you meet Mike Bevans is very close to the truth. A veteran of many years' hotel experience, he gives the impression that he considers himself lucky to have ended up owning such a magical place, and his enthusiasm for his little patch of paradise is infectious.

I have a theory with hotels, which is that the personality of the chief is responsible for the general ambience. Sure it's important that rooms are spacious and well-equipped, contemporary and comfortable (which they are), and of course it's always a bonus if the food is good (which it is), but the attitude of the boss is often mirrored by the staff. The most beautiful place in the world can easily be ruined by people who don't make you feel welcome, and in this respect Linthwaite House is as exceptional as the view.

Interestingly, from Bevans's point of view, the view has never been better. With warmer temperatures it is now possible to enjoy the outdoor terrace for longer, but also because water-skiing is no longer allowed on the lake.

From the terrace you have one of the best views of Lake Windermere – the largest lake in England.

In winter, it's still possible to enjoy the beautiful surroundings from the orangerie.

The dining room, red and cosy, is recognized as one of the best in the Lake District.

Surprisingly modern, the suites at nthwaite House are a successful mix of modern, classic and cosy.

Croquet fields, putting greens, salmon-fishing – Linthwaite House has plenty to offer guests who never want to leave the premises.

The terrace, with its amazing view, is popular for lunch, dinner and drinks from May to October.

It might seem strange that not being able to water-ski on a lake so well-suited to it would be a plus, but in the height of summer, Lake Windermere used to be a chopped-up mess with countless boats zig-zagging over its expanse, and more and more jet skis adding to irritating levels of high-pitch engine noise. Since they were all banned, the lake has gone back to tranquillity – and on a windless day the mirror-like surface remains unbroken. It's a bit sad perhaps for the extremely well-equipped water-skiing club on Windermere, and I'm sure members who now commute to the nearby coast to practice their sport aren't thrilled.

But Bevans is far from nostalgic for the days of skiing on the lake. Indeed he is delighted by the return to nature. And it's not as if there's a shortage of activities to fill the void. Apart from hiking, the area's most popular pursuit, Linthwaite House offers flyfishing in their own tarn, croquet on the lawn, and honing your short-game skills on the putting greens. But without a doubt, the favoured activity is sitting on the terrace, or in the conservatory in less idyllic weather, and gazing out at the view. Fifteen years later, Bevans still gets a kick out of his view because, as he will tell you, it's never the same twice.

address Crook Road, Windermere, LA23 3JA **email** stay@linthwaite.com
telephone +44 (0)1539 488600 **fax** +44 (0)1539 488601
room rates from £176

the samling

In the early 1780s a gentleman named Edward Thorneycroft was so taken by the beauty of Lake Windermere that he built a house on what is arguably its finest vantage point. Located several hundred feet above the lake on its north-eastern shore, the house was an historic anomaly because it was built for no other reason than the view from it and indeed of it. It was not an investment, there was no farm or pub or other possible rental income. It was constructed purely for reasons of aesthetic enjoyment, and as such it embodied the emerging desirability of the Lake District as a holiday destination.

The house was called The Samling, and it is not just the name that remains unchanged to this day. It still enjoys one of the best vistas of the lake, and is still surrounded by the original parcel of sixty-four acres of wild flowers, woodland, garden and fields. Granted there are rather more visitors to the lakes these days, and tour buses often clog the skinny roads in summer, but with the odd exception of a pier here and a pub there, the beauty of the landscape is intact. It is this beauty that was immortalized by the poet William Wordsworth. Born in Cumbria, the aptly named Wordsworth became preoccupied with the conviction that man was at his best and purest when close to nature. It was only logical then that he should have installed himself in a cottage in the Lake District rented from a certain John Benson, the proprietor of The Samling.

Even after Wordsworth moved out, the literary connection was maintained by the next tenant, Thomas de Quincey, author of *Confessions of an English Opium Eater*, and later by Miss Weeton, a governess to the family who was renting The Samling, and who wrote her gripping *Journal of a Governess – An Exposé of Life in a Tyrannised Georgian Era Household*. The poet laureate Robert Southey also spent time at the lakes, as did Samuel Taylor Coleridge, the best friend of Wordsworth. Collectively known as The Lakes Poets, these writers helped to popularize the area with their literary work, not to mention the impact of Wordsworth's bestselling *Guide to the Lakes*.

Simply put, The Samling continues the well-established local tradition of appreciation of the landscape, except that this is possible today in the seclusion and exclusivity of The Samling estate. The entire set-up is geared to create the impression that for the duration of your visit, the house is yours for your own exclusive enjoyment. And if privacy and space are the new luxury, then The Samling certainly is luxurious with a capital 'L'.

The rooms are like apartments, the dining room will never serve more than a dozen in one space at a time, and the bar is one where you simply help yourself and keep your own tab. With possibly the most magnificently placed hot tub in all of the UK, a croquet lawn, professional meeting rooms for small conferences in the stables, space to sit sixty in the old Dutch barn, and Lake Windermere at the bottom of the drive, this is not a place that is short on facilities or things to do. Riding in the morning, sailing in the afternoon, trout-fishing before dinner, canoeing to an island in the lake, sunset in the hot tub, diving in for a pre-breakfast swim – all is simply a matter of asking the staff, or doing it yourself. The Samling makes a point of defining itself as a house in the country, not a country house hotel. It's supposed to be relaxed and informal, and the contemporary unpretentious interiors certainly contribute to this ambience. No wonder then that the hotel's own literature insists that 'You can't stop The Samling from making you feel different.'

address Ambleside Road, Windermere, LA23 1LR **email** info@thesamling.com

telephone +44 (0)1539 431922 **fax** +44 (0)1539 430400

room rates from £195

the scottish highlands

Barren, bare, but hauntingly beautiful, the lochs and mountains of northern Scotland are like no other place on earth. This is an area positively primordial in its make up: devoid of trees, covered in shiny green moss, and dotted with rugged brooks, rivers and streams that light up like silver ribbons when the odd shaft of light pierces through the swirling clouds of dark grey mist. It's the kind of place that makes you want to put on a woollen kilt, a rough linen shirt and a big sweater, then drink a few wee drams of single malt in a stone shack, and end up doing the Highland Fling on a straw-covered floor of a 'black' house with a wild raven-haired lassie.

Then there are the castles; dark brooding piles of lichen-covered stone sitting majestically in the most mesmerizing locations aside wind-blown lochs. As a result of constant clashes between warring clans over centuries, many are in a state of ruin, and controversially they are kept that way by Scottish Heritage partly because this is how they were famously painted by many of Great Britain's best known landscape artists during the 19th and early 20th centuries.

The barren nature of this wonderful wilderness is accentuated even more by the absence of people. There are few villages and towns, and most of the countryside is inhabited only by sheep – which, by the way, is no accident. Triggered by the Napoleonic Wars which sent the price of wool skyrocketing, the landlords of the Highlands forcibly moved a lot of their tenants to coastal towns, leaving more fertile land for the sheep. Eventually the price of wool collapsed, but by then the absence of tenant farmers meant the wildlife population had regenerated in such numbers that it could sustain even the most lavish of shooting parties – an aristocratic tradition that continues to this day. And tradition is a key part of the Highlands' appeal. Despite the displacement of its ancient communities, this is an area that has managed to keep many of its traditions. Think of a Scottish icon, whether it be tartan bearing the distinctive checks and colours of the ancient clans; Harris Tweed, handwoven by the islanders of the Outer Hebrides; single malt whisky from places such as Oban; and of course hunting, shooting and fishing – all of these originate and flourish in the Highlands.

inverlochy castle

There are two Inverlochy Castles. One is a dark, brooding pile of lichen-covered stone, rising ominously from a strategic position on wind-blown Loch Linnhe. It features prominently in Scottish medieval history as the venue for the Battles of Inverlochy in 1431 and 1645, but was then destroyed by the Campbells' retreating army in 1645 and remains a ruin to this day.

The Inverlochy Castle that now operates as a hotel was built in 1863 by the first Lord Abinger, an enthusiastic outdoorsman and globe-trotting hunter. Some of his 'kills', testament to his passion, still decorate the billiard room, with pride of place given to a trio of huge stags that are identified as having been shot in Jackson Hole, Wyoming. Travelling to places such as Africa and the American Rocky Mountains certainly qualified as exotic in those days, and apparently Lord Abinger was no less adventurous with his choice of house guests. One famous political figure who wrote glowing letters back to his wife in America about the extraordinary Highlands landscape in the summer was Jefferson Davis – the first elected president of the Confederate Republic of the American South (who only held office for eighteen months before the South was defeated).

Far less controversial was a visit by Queen Victoria, who in September 1873 spent a week sketching and painting at Inverlochy Castle. 'I never saw a lovelier or more romantic spot' was what she wrote in her diaries, and to this day these words sum up the appeal of this castle very well.

Framed by Ben Nevis, Scotland's highest peak, and surrounded by emerald-green forests, the setting is an ever changing series of postcard-like vistas, even though this castle, unlike the original Inverlochy, is not actually on a loch. But Lord Abinger was clearly a man who knew what he wanted, and Inverlochy's location is ideal for any fan of shooting, hunting and fishing.

It's true that even in the middle of summer the weather can be quite cold and blustery, but in a way that only adds to the appeal of this neo-Gothic pile. With a huge double-storey volume and grand fireplaces that burn whenever guests are in residence, the contrast between the cosy baronial old world interior and the rugged outdoors of the Scottish Highlands is exactly what guests want – as was confirmed when Inverlochy Castle was voted as the best hotel in Europe in 2006 by readers of the American magazine *Travel & Leisure*.

Until 1969 Inverlochy remained a private residence, and yet even when it was converted to a hotel it has managed to remain that baronial ambience that one hopes to find in the Highlands. You won't see the staff wearing kilts or anything too predictably Scottish, but you do have to have the traditional porridge followed by scrambled eggs and salmon for breakfast. Its strength is the fact that the proportions and internal architecture remain virtually untouched. It still looks every bit a castle on the outside, and the same is true for the interior. These days far fewer royal guests arrive for visits, but it's fascinating to consider that you can stay in the very same suite where Queen Victoria once dumped her easels and oils in the corner.

The Highlands are dotted with extraordinary castles in dramatic settings, but many are abandoned and in various states of ruin. I met an architect from Edinburgh in the old fishing town of Gairloch who explained the anomaly of Scottish castles. Obsessed with these ancient fortresses, he had documented just about all of them and explained that although many of the most beautiful and impressive are in a state of ruin, Scottish Heritage actively choose to keep them that way. This means that even though there is no shortage of people lining up to take on renovation and restoration, they are simply not allowed to do so. Hence the fact that in a countryside full of medieval castles, there are very few that are habitable. That alone makes Inverlochy unique.

address Torlundy, Fort William, PH33 6SN **email** info@inverlochycastlehotel.com

telephone +44 (0)1397 702177 **fax** +44 (0)1397 702953

room rates from £300

pool house hotel

Situated on the water's edge in Poolewe, a tiny hamlet just five minutes north of Gairloch on the far north-west coast of Scotland, Pool House Hotel looks like your typical north Scottish coastal dwelling. Whitewashed stone and a roof of tiled slate, it is essentially a large version of a typical whitewashed cottage. Inside it's a different story.

Other hotel proprietors in the area will volunteer that the standard of Pool House Hotel's interiors is exceptional, and they are right. The result of fifteen years' work, Pool House took the brave step of reducing the number of rooms to create apartments, and as Margaret the owner will tell you with a slight 'what were we doing?' shaking of the head, 'We took a hotel with twenty-odd rooms and turned it into a place with just five', six if you count the newly converted boathouse.

In fact rooms is a word they studiously avoid; these are suites – but that being such an overused word in the hotel game, perhaps apartment is better. Each one follows a different theme. The most unexpected is the Diadem apartment, designed to mimic the style and opulence of a first-class cabin on the Titanic. Decorated with memorabilia from the ill-fated Transatlantic liner, it is not a room for the superstitious. For lovers of opulent Victoriana,

there's the Campania suite – housed in the original residential apartment of Osgood Mackenzie (creator of nearby Inverewe Gardens), its four-poster bed, canopied bath and fireplace are fine 130-year-old examples of period fantasy and decorative indulgence. They also have a French empire apartment: the Achates, in black and gold, not to mention the Nairana, an apartment inspired by the grand palaces of Rajasthan. In keeping with this decadent level of luxury, Pool House Hotel boasts a bar big enough for a full-sized billiards table, a very popular restaurant and a cosy chintzy library in which you could not possibly find space for one more bibelot.

Without a doubt, some of the most dramatic coastline of the world is to be found here in the far north-west of Scotland. Big, sweeping crescents of bleached sand, framed by huge mountainside chunks of grey granite partially covered in moss, appear every now and then around the next majestic bend of a coastal road that takes in a view of the distant islands of the Hebrides. For surfers, there's even a half-decent wave every now and then, though even with the warming effects of the Gulf Stream, few would contemplate going into the water without a wetsuit.

It may not have Mediterranean weather, but the sheer drama of the landscape more than compensates for the unlikely occurrence of getting a suntan. What's more, there are more villages here on the coast than in the rest of the Highlands. This is because during the Highland Clearances, many of the inhabitants of the Highland pastures (those who didn't emigrate) were relocated to villages on the coast. This means you're more likely to get a good meal in these parts. All the local seafood comes straight off the boats, and that includes sole, monkfish, langoustine and crab.

That said, a hotel like Pool House still comes as a bit of a surprise. The latest addition, Whimbrel, is a former boathouse reinvented as a cathedral-ceilinged cottage for two, not more than ten feet from the sea. All of this may seem a bizarre melange in a tiny hamlet opposite the Hebrides, but eccentricity and drama have plenty of precedent here. This is where Osgood Mackenzie chose to create his semi-tropical gardens in the benign micro-climate created by the Gulf Stream – but where nonetheless the weather is constantly busy creating the kind of drama worthy of *Hamlet*.

address   Highland, Poolewe, Ross-shire, IV22 2LD   **email**   enquiries@poolhousehotel.com

telephone   +44 (0)1445 781272   **fax**   +44 (0)1445 781403

room rates   from £200

boath house

Boath House is a jewel; an architectural rarity. A Georgian house designed in the classical neo-Palladian model but on a more approachable scale. There were never many of these stone gems built, and certainly not in the smaller scale of Boath. I've come across one or two, particularly in Ireland, but this is the first small Palladian Georgian mansion that I know of in the UK that has been turned into a hotel.

Luckily, apart from saving it from certain ruin, Don and Wendy Matheson did nothing to affect the classical attributes of the architecture, inside or out. Boath House, often described as the most beautiful Regency house in Scotland, was built in 1825 for Sir James Dunbar by architect Archibald Simpson of Aberdeen, whose portrait still hangs in the upper hall. The Dunbar family lived here until 1923. The twenty-odd acres of gardens, which include a very picturesque lake and a formal walled kitchen garden, predate even the Georgian house; they belonged to a mansion which had occupied this ground since the mid-1500s.

As was the custom of the day, the kitchens were originally in the basement. This space has now been cleverly converted to a spa and fitness centre. Equally unintrusive, the butler's pantry at the foot of the stairs is now the ladies powder room. Apart from that, not much has changed, aside from the fact that the bathroom of Room 3 now occupies what used to be an entire guest room, and Lady Dunbar's downstairs bedroom is now the kitchen. But not one wall, door or doorway has been altered, and that's the big attraction of Boath House: it operates as a hotel, but first and foremost it remains a splendid home. Because there are only six rooms – seven if you count the separate cottage – there will not be more than fourteen people in residence at any one time, and considering the dozen or so people that work at Boath House, there's a ratio of staff to guest reminiscent of Georgian times.

It is, for all intents and purposes, an early 19th-century house with an early 19th-century sensibility, yet in respect to things that are important, modern standards apply. Take for example the bathrooms. All are capacious and modern with lots of daylight, and if you're lucky enough to stay in Room 3, then you will luxuriate in a twenty-by-twenty-foot space with a pair of claw-footed baths set side-by-side on a raised platform in the middle of the room to provide bathers with a view through Georgian windows over the weeping willows and the lake.

The red dining room on the ground floor opens directly onto the lawns that lead down to the swan pond.

Symmetry is one of the hallmarks of Georgian houses, inspired by the Veneto master – Andrea Palladio.

The garden is one of the highlights – th so acres of swan ponds, weeping will sweeping lawns and the odd folly.

est rooms are all completely different, some classic and white, others dark and funky.

Some of the bathrooms are larger than most hotel rooms. The bath in Room 3 has 'his and hers' claw-foot baths and a view of the garden

A neo-Palladian Georgian-era jewel in stone – Boath is recognized as the finest Regency house in this part of Scotland.

The design merit of Boath is clear, but the question remains; why Nairn? With so much on offer in the Highlands, why would one venture to the coastal plains that flank Scotland's impressive mountains? The answer is simple: golf.

Situated on the Moray Firth, just north-west of Inverness, this is an area of sweeping sand dunes and broad stretches of beach: exactly the kind of countryside that gave birth to the game in the first place. The Royal Nairn golf links are not as famous as those in St Andrews, but it is certainly recognized as one of the best courses in Scotland, with the added plus that the front nine all play along the coast. It's what is known as a links course, where the bunkers are a reminder that the first sand traps were naturally occurring sand dunes adjoining grass fairways. Plus, being north of Inverness means this is a place where you can go out mid-summer for a round of eighteen holes after dinner and still be back before dark.

Not that playing 'the game' is essential to enjoying the hotel or the setting. Facing north, Nairn has similar beaches to the ones in North Norfolk – huge wide stretches of fine sand, an abundance of dolphins and even the odd whale. With just six rooms and a separate guest house in the garden, it's possible to book the entire place, as a whole bunch of German pilots did recently, landing their light aircraft on Boath's immaculate lawns. Try doing that at St Andrews.

address Auldearn, Nairn, IV12 5TE **email** wendy@boath-house.com

telephone +44 (0)1667 454896 **fax** +44 (0)1667 455469

room rates from £190

kinnaird estate

Situated on 9,000 acres of prime 'sporting' real estate, Kinnaird is a paradise for people who love to fish or to shoot. Located just south of Blair Castle, the historic seat of Lord Athol's enormous 250,000-acre estate, Kinnaird is nestled into the eastern corner of the Scottish Highlands, a very different landscape from the lochs and moss-covered mountains of the north-west.

This is a rich land, covered in forests of old oak and massive conifers. Historically it is recognized as the cradle of Scottish forestry, a result of the passions of Lord Athol, who kicked off his interest in forestry by planting four larch trees next to the cathedral at Dunkeld – trees that have protected status today as well as being credited as the great granddaddies of Scotland's beautiful larch trees.

And through the middle of these forested mountains runs the river Tay, a broad, blue, fast-running ribbon that has yielded some record-weight salmon caught by flyfishing. In fact the record was held by Lady Mary Marsh of Kinnaird, a formidable woman who could often be found snapping her rod from a boat in the dead of winter. Her record catch, a beast of forty-five pounds, is mounted in a glass box in the billiard room. Then, one weekend, her niece Lettice

Marsh caught a forty-eight-pound monster during a short visit. Sad as she may have been to lose the record, Lady Marsh surely would have been proud that it went to another woman.

Even today, the estate still employs a master of the fishing called a *ghillie*, whose task it is to help the angler increase the odds in his favour – the submarine equivalent of a stalker. What is clear from Kinnaird is that its credentials as a sporting estate are longstanding and without pretension. The framed pictures in the Cedar Lounge (so-named because it's panelled in cedar) or in the classic billiards room with its view of the river, attests to the pedigree of this estate as a destination for keen sportsmen. Prince Charles et al are depicted in wading kit or shooting tweeds, and it's easy to imagine the house full of rosy-cheeked outdoorsy aristo-types, boosted in their pursuits by a good red and plenty of single malt.

Yet despite having converted to a hotel, this 'weekend shooting party' atmosphere survives. You may be a paying guest, but you feel like a house guest. That's because as imposing as the Edwardian stone pile may be, with its incomparable location beside the fast-flowing River Tay, it doesn't give the impression of trying too hard.

The billiards room enjoys a splendid view of the River Tay, and the walls are decorated with record-breaking salmon caught by the family.

Louis XV-style chinoiserie hand-painted panels give the dining room a soft feminine elegance – an unexpected touch for a shooting estate.

Each guest room enjoys a view, whether the splendid gardens or the river valley, densely wooded forest behind the prop

...eeping with the low-key origins of the
...e as a family home, the guest rooms are
...'shabby chic' aristocratic interiors.

The library – a dark handsome affair
decorated in tobacco tones – is used
as a venue for private dinners.

Some of the guest rooms are housed in the
old stable blocks – a more private alternative
to the main house, with a view of the river.

Kinnaird has mastered the kind of understated luxury that used to define the truly authentic country estates. The guest rooms are a good example. They are very comfortable, but they are not overly new or too slick. They are homey, a bit shabby even – which is how traditionally they would have been.

Atmosphere is a tricky thing to try to describe, but that's exactly what Kinnaird has in spades.

It's not the most sophisticated or elaborate estate in Scotland, but it could well be the most inviting. I am not really a fishing or shooting enthusiast, but a place like Kinnaird makes me wish I was. Plus it's not every day you discover a spot that looks like a set from *A River Runs Through It*, and gives you the chance, for once, to tell the truth when you say that the one that got away was 'this big'.

address Dunkeld, Perthshire, PH8 0LB **email** enquiry@kinnairdestate.com

telephone +44 (0)1796 482440 **fax** +44 (0)1796 482289

room rates from £275

First published in the United Kingdom in 2007 by Thames & Hudson Ltd,
181A High Holborn, London WC1V 7QX

www.thamesandhudson.com

© 2007 Hip Hotels Media Ltd

British Library Cataloguing-in-Publication Data
A catalogue record for this book is available from the British Library

ISBN-13: 978-0-500-28678-4
ISBN-10: 0-500-28678-7

Printed and bound in Singapore by CS Graphics

Designed by Maggi Smith